Reverent Whisper

Chetna Asmi

BALBOA.
PRESS

A DIVISION OF HAY HOUSE

Balboa Press books may be ordered through booksellers or by contacting:

Balboa Press
A Division of Hay House
1663 Liberty Drive
Bloomington, IN 47403
www.balboapress.com.au
1 (877) 407-4847

Because of the dynamic nature of the Internet, any web addresses or
links contained in this book may have changed since publication and
may no longer be valid. The views expressed in this work are solely those
of the author and do not necessarily reflect the views of the publisher,
and the publisher hereby disclaims any responsibility for them.

The author of this book does not dispense medical advice or prescribe
the use of any technique as a form of treatment for physical, emotional,
or medical problems without the advice of a physician, either directly
or indirectly. The intent of the author is only to offer information
of a general nature to help you in your quest for emotional and
spiritual well-being. In the event you use any of the information in
this book for yourself, which is your constitutional right, the author
and the publisher assume no responsibility for your actions.

Any people depicted in stock imagery provided by Getty Images are
models, and such images are being used for illustrative purposes only.
Certain stock imagery © Getty Images.

Print information available on the last page.

ISBN: 978-1-5043-1727-6 (sc)
ISBN: 978-1-5043-1728-3 (e)

Balboa Press rev. date: 03/22/2019

Introduction

Something has given me not only the opportunity, but the know-how and the wisdom to write this book, even though I have had limited education in the field of literature. In actual fact, I've had limited education in all academic matters, leaving school at the age of fifteen with what you could call average grades at best.

This simple man's text has been written in response to a calling, for the want of a better term. It has never been my intention to write or to be a writer, for that matter, so I feel blessed to have discovered a part of myself that lay dormant for the first forty-nine years of my life. Now, at the age of fifty-seven, I find myself in a maze of magic and mystery, within my own mind.

It all began with an awakening of an extraordinary kind, the something, which coincided with the acquisition of my computer and the discovery of Microsoft Word (with spellcheck, of course). When I was a teenager at school and beyond, I was always in awe of people who had written books. I thought all authors must be highly intelligent, with many years of study behind them. This is true in a lot of cases, but it never occurred to me that books could be written by anyone with a story or an imagination, even someone with a limited education.

It has taken many years for me to find out why this has happened to me, what my role is, what I need to do, and how I am to go about it. If the truth be known, I still have no idea what I am doing, but as a friend once said, "Fake it till you make it."

I now find myself thrust upon a voyage of self-knowledge, without warning and without a handbook. As those before me can attest, it is an exhilarating ride, like an endless roller-coaster ride into the deep unknown. It's a trip every single human being will eventually have to take, but it's not for me to say when. It will happen when they're ready, but it best happen soon, for the survival of all humanity is at stake. It is a trek into the truth, an extreme adventure that will not disappoint.

Several months ago, as my magical mind was wandering through its maze of mystery, I experienced a profound revelation. I felt myself step into my greatness and immediately realised my genius, almost some sort of divine entity. Well, almost. I remember saying to myself, "Oh, my God, what next?" Then I heard God whisper, "Back off." If the truth be known, God would probably say, "Welcome to my world."

Now if you knew what I had endured, or at least put myself through, for the first forty-nine years of my life, you too would be wondering why this sudden eruption of self-belief has shown itself after being missing for so long. And furthermore, what was I going to do with this new-found creative genius that had suddenly popped up from within? Was I to save the world?

Well, it's funny you mention that because that is exactly the burden placed upon me. I call it a burden because I have no idea how to go about saving the world. My portfolio of magic and mystery has let me down badly in this area. Yet I feel this overwhelming responsibility to find out what it takes. I must have the tools at hand; otherwise, this somewhat mammoth task wouldn't have been bestowed upon me, would it?

What sort of tool is needed, and when will it appear? Is this keyboard that I'm pounding the answer? Are the words that appear on my computer screen the answer? I'm just getting over the realisation that I'm a genius, and I instantly have to come up with a plan to save the world. What if we're not meant to save the world? Okay, stupid question; just seeing if I still had your attention.

I don't know the exact numbers, but I'd say there have been hundreds of thousands of people over hundreds of years who have either written books, stood on soapboxes, made movies, or even fought wars, all with the intention of saving the world. Who wonders (or even cares, for that matter) if they made a difference? Is the world a better place because of their efforts? Even today, there are people lending their creative skills, and their hard-earned dollars, with the sole intent of making this a better world to live in. Are we listening? Are we really listening?

I stopped for a moment to listen, and I could hear the people's call for peace, freedom, civil rights, the saving of the whales, and the saving of the rainforests and its tigers and orangutans. There's issues with global warming, pollution, the ozone layer, famine, sickness, addictions, discrimination. There's corruption, rape, murder, and mental illness.

This was all too far from where I was at. I felt too close to myself to leave the comfort of my own peace and happiness. I was too entrenched doing battle with my own mind every time it wandered into dark places, let alone trying to fix other people's fetishes and faults. Maybe the wealthy and civilised countries of the world could form a committee to address most of these issues, so that government policies would benefit the world and the people, plants, and animals to come.

Just give me a mandate, people, and an appropriate budget, and I'll show you what needs to be done. The first two places on earth I'd start would be the Vatican City and the jungles of Colombo.

I just had a thought: Maybe I could sit at home and meditate on love and peace, and then project it out into the world. It would save having to climb a soapbox, or make movies, or even write a book. I'd also avoid good Lords and drug lords.

I read somewhere that there are only two significant influences of great importance in the world: the subconscious mind and God, and everything else was created by them. Well, that narrows it down; I'll just toss a coin. Two of the most powerful things known to humanity, and I'm expected to do battle with them. I think I'll leave God till last, 'cause when I'm done with the subconscious mind, He might feel intimidated and surrender to me.

My genius has just come to the fore. I know exactly what needs to be done. I'll write a biography about some fictitious character, who thinks he has all the answers. If he fails, you can all blame him, and if he succeeds, you can thank me.

Chapter 1

Hi. I'm fictitious. You can call me ... let's say ... umm ... James. Yes, James. James Semper Digne. The name reminds me of my high school days and has a significant meaning or translation, whichever way you want to look at it. I think it's Spanish or something, but who cares? It's just a name. And what's in a name, right?

My mother was a schoolteacher for a short while before she eloped with my dad. I heard she was thrilled when she changed her name from Miss Pope to Mrs Digne (pronounce it "Dine" if you are having problems with it). None of my older siblings have a stupid middle name like Semper, but she said she always liked that word, as it had a special meaning. Why it took her till her seventh child to find the courage to use it, I don't know. She said that she was waiting for someone special to come along.

Well, that's what she told me.

You can call me Jim or Jimmy. I also answer to Dingers or Dingo, which my mates used to call me. I'm an intelligent person but definitely not an academic, intellectual type. I'm closer to simple, yet I can be complex, humble, and of course, extraordinary. I'm not narcissistic, but I have suffered from the occasional personality malfunction, which I used to think were just moody moments. I've been described at times as an unusual character, but I've never let that deter me. If I thought I was usual, then I'd be worried. So as you can see, I'm pretty normal and basically a good guy.

The author of this book has created me so he can shirk his responsibility of having to save the world. Personally, I think he's a little naive, even ignorant, if he thinks we can save this world. I just hope he does me justice, you know, and makes me out to be the good guy.

I'm not sure why he chose someone like me, because I don't really give a damn whether we save the world or not. The planet will keep evolving whether we're here or not. In fact, the planet would be better off without us. The human species will always find a way to adapt to the changing planet, even if we do become mutant versions of ourselves.

What's annoying is that this present society of human is so primitive compared to past advanced civilisations and highly evolved beings, yet we are categorised as an intelligent species. We couldn't live without the planet, but the planet would prosper without us; the human race is destroying the very thing it calls home. The dilemma is this: does saving the world mean saving humankind from pain and suffering, or does it mean saving the planet from human destruction?

If, in fact, my role is to help save the planet, then I would advise that we eliminate the human race, which would ensure the planet's survival. Being a fictitious person, born out of the thought of one human being's unstable subconscious, and chosen to save the world, it seems logical that I get to select the direction to take, without persecution. One cannot crucify a fictitious person.

One can only assume that if one were to save humankind, there is no guarantee that the planet would be saved. However, in the process of saving humankind, one would hope that humankind would gain the wisdom and the know-how necessary to save the planet. It all seems so simple to me, or am I just a freak of nature? Am I a reincarnation from an ancient civilization that lived amongst highly evolved beings? It seems obvious to me that one's role is to save humankind from itself by instilling the wisdom and self-knowledge necessary to avoid self-destruction. That should not be too difficult with my obvious wisdom, self-knowledge, and lack of intellectual logic.

Due to the confusion around the worshipping of gods, goddesses, and God the Creator over the centuries, and the many differing religions, philosophies, and beliefs, I have been given instructions to stay away from God, in any form, for the time being. A belief has been instilled in me that if I start writing too much about God, then my keyboard will explode.

It seems that what has created the world is not the one that is to save the world. I have been chosen for that role, and as the pages roll on, you will find that "I" means you, us, and them. *Everyone.* The person who has given me this fictitious opportunity has obviously done his homework. He knows full well that saving the world begins and ends with that other great power: the human mind. This includes the unconscious, subconscious, conscious, and superconscious, and the most important extension of all these is consciousness. This is where the intellect falls down and the simple human will reign supreme.

My research into this complex and fascinating area of one's existence—the mind—tells me that most people in the world are psychologically challenged, unstable, or disturbed, which means they'll understand everything I say. The only people who may struggle to keep up here are the intellectuals, as a mental challenge to them means they need to do more research. They will always be in denial of their handicap because their minds have convinced them they are beyond reproach in this part of their anatomy. I also know that the intellectual mind will take us farther from the truth of who we are. It has to. It is too easily programmed to explore the outside world, which as all of us wise people know is a reflection of our inner world.

When you know your self, you know everything. Imagine when everyone eventually wakes up to this fact. Imagine.

There is also the adage that a healthy mind breeds healthy thoughts and, thus, a healthy body. Does this mean we are unhealthy because we are psychologically challenged? Of course it does, people. Of course, it does. I ain't no intellectual, but I sure knows that. Let's get some scientific research done in this area—not to prove me wrong but to spend some subsidies in the right areas of research.

I read somewhere that if you write out your life story; it can help to find meaning in your life, which in turn makes for a better world. It might even save the world. Do you get my drift? It doesn't matter how insignificant you think your life has been. If you collect all the experiences and write them down, and then you are able to make sense of them, they will tell you who you were, who you are, who you are not, and who you are going to be.

"How can this possibly help?" I hear you ask. I have no idea. But if I am going to conquer the subconscious mind, I have to start somewhere.

I know that not everyone will have the time to write their stuff down, for whatever reason, but that's okay. That's what I'm here for; if I write all my stuff down, I know yours wouldn't be much different. After all, we're all as crazy as each other, in some way, and we're going to have to save the world together. So I figure if I can be one with my mind, I can be one with everyone's mind. It's a hunch, and it's all I have to go on right now.

A lot of my story will be of others' experiences as well as my own. In fact, I will use their experiences as my own so that it seems like I have had an interesting life. Kind of like my fiction and their fact told in my story. Don't dwell on it. Just keep reading. It will be deep and shallow, vast and narrow. I love contradictions. The metaphysical mind laps them up, while the logical mind goes nuts, wanting to know, "Well, which one is it? It can't be both. It's either deep or shallow, vast or narrow."

It can be described as metaphysical madness, people. Here comes a story that is fictitious fact.

Chapter 2

I don't remember coming into this world, which is probably—or is it "pre baby"?—a good thing. Having researched pre-baby (as in foetus in the womb) recently, I have been informed that my learning began well before that magical moment of childbirth.

The baby can be influenced by many things whilst in the foetal stage, which makes the parenting stage begin well before the baby is born. During pregnancy would be a great time to teach a child how to save the world. It would be like a mobile class womb. The foetus could be read positive affirmations and sung melodious mantras, with chanting and meditation music. Actually, that's not as silly as it sounds. We could have indigo children running around everywhere while teaching us things like love, peace, and happiness.

Of course, there is the question of reincarnation to contend with. This means the foetus may be carrying baggage from a past life or two—or more. Well, that just ruined my idea of the flower children revolution. I suppose one way to deal with the reincarnates is to get them before they leave the planet. One could go to all the aged care facilities and decode their programmed minds. We could have movies on self-knowledge and universal truths playing all day long. Or we could plug in an iPod full of great philosophers, mystics, and yogis of our time, men like Gandhi, Mandela, the Dalai Lama, Sai Baba, Yogananda, Aquinas, Confucius, Descartes, Aristotle, Plato, and James Digne, to name a few.

The problem there, of course, is that the oldies may not want to leave, and who'd blame them? Finding out the truth would be the revival they've been waiting for all their lives. We'd end up with old, grey, nomad hippies who would want to prance around naked all day. Some may even want to indulge in some old-fashioned sex (or is that old sex?). I may have just touched on the tool for saving the world (or is *stumbled* more appropriate?).

My research into childbirth also informed me that the two things a newborn fears are loud noise and falling. All I can say about this is that if chanting is an option, keep it down a bit. If I was a newborn, though, I'd like peace and quiet, the only sounds being my mother's heart beating, her breath, and her soft voice. That would be the voice I'd be accustomed to, and her sounds would be comforting. The other thing would be the bonding, staying attached and suckling for as long as possible, our bodies not separating during the whole experience, from the womb to the breast, with the only touch being my mother's. My instincts would be fine-tuned to the point where silence, no separation (no sense of falling), and give me something to eat is all that I'd need in those precious minutes upon entering this magical place we call earth.

I would really like to go back there to experience what it was like, you know, being born with awareness, and as soon as I was able to talk, I'd let the adults know what it was like. I don't think I'd appreciate that needle, but they're harmless, or are we being duped here too? That's another story, and the truth will be revealed in time.

It's all hypothetical, though, and probably a little hypocritical as well. But still, a lot more education could be of great help to many parents of unborn children, and not just around the effects of the foetus during pregnancy, but around the lovemaking process that leads to the pregnancy. In fact, it is a crucial area of learning, from penis to placenta, and there is lots of literature on the subject out there. So go learn it and help me to help us save the world.

I'm not here to give you expert advice on any particular subject. However, I would like you to introduce yourself to Guru Swami Google, who can assist you with information on any subject in the world.

I have this question I ask myself from time to time: If every person in the world thought how I thought, said what I said, and did what I did, would the world be a better place? The man I am today is because of the man I was yesterday; am I a better man today than I was yesterday? One's attitude towards oneself reflects upon those around one. But I haven't always been perfect.

There is not a conscious mind that can remember childbirth, and I've often wondered at what age we start holding on to memories. I mean, do we remember being two years old when we are three years old? I guess that part of life is irrelevant, or is it? However, we never forget that which we've remembered, even though we don't remember. What I mean here is, surely all our memories are stored in our subconscious mind, which means they are always there. However, because we are so young and our brain has not developed to the stage where it can hold memories, we simply forget, yet the memories are still there. In fact, are they memories at all? Could they not be called impressions, feelings, emotions, scars, or even trauma left by an experience? This is getting a bit heavy for me, so I'll move on, but don't forget this paragraph. It could be a vital clue into the behaviour of the human race.

The earliest age that I can remember was around three years old. Unfortunately, there aren't too many memories of my toddler years, but I'm sure I had a wonderful time. My first recollection of life was the time I chewed and swallowed what I thought was a lolly, which I'd found behind the couch. We were moving house, which I also remember, and when the couch was moved, I pounced, as you would when you see a lolly at that age. The fact that there were seven other kids around, all under twelve years of age, made the matter a little more urgent, not to mention my competitive nature in claiming victory by getting there first. However, it made me ill, the pill that is, and I couldn't keep it down, which was probably a good thing. It was the size of a contraceptive pill, but it certainly could not have been that, for obvious reasons.

I do remember also waiting on the side of the road near our house for a bus. My mother would dress us up and take us to church with her. Having had a religious upbringing herself, I guess she felt obliged to expose us to the wonders of God. I don't recall that ritual lasting very long, as I don't recall being over the moon about being preached to. I always thought that Jesus was an interesting character, though.

So at the age of three years old, I can only remember a few things. Was life that dull? Why don't I remember my little brother? Where were my one sister and five older brothers? They sure left an impression. I still can't remember much before five and a half years of age, when I started school. I know there were a lot of kin around, but I don't remember any, not one experience with any of them. The only other things I can remember between three and five were the times my dad would take me with him to milk the cow, and that I was a super shy child. I would hang onto my mother's skirt for what seemed all day, and I would hide under the dining table other times. I couldn't cope with any visitors and would hide under that table, which was always adorned with a tablecloth that hung halfway to the floor. That's all I can remember, and I've been trying for over fifty years to remember more.

The point I'm making, and the question is (and this goes for everyone), where are all the memories of every day and night for five years? Do they just disappear? Are they hidden deep in our subconscious mind, and were we psychologically affected by any of the experiences that we don't remember?

I have a scar between my eyes from a wound I received after falling on the corner of that dining table. I can only imagine the fright I would have got, the state of panic my mother would have experienced, the blood, the doctor, the stitches, and the healing time. I don't remember anything about it. My mother spent years trying to convince me that it really happened, as I couldn't understand how something so serious could not be remembered, no matter what age I was.

What I'm doing here is building the foundation of a story, our life story. For it is in our life story, yours and mine, that we can eventually find a way of saving the world. I did a little research; due to a phenomenon called infantile amnesia, it is not possible for children under the age of three to hold on to memories, as that part of the brain system is not adequately developed. Older children are able to hold onto some memories as their brain develops. The real question is, does our subconscious mind know the secrets of our first five years, and do the thoughts/ memories/experiences/scars of this period influence our life? Hold that thought. We may be onto something here, so we'll come back to it, if I remember.

I'm hovering around this age bracket for personal reasons. I've dealt with the major issues from the age of five onwards (well, all those that I can remember, anyway), but it's hard to deal with issues that you don't remember, and if you don't remember them, then why are they issues?

The real reasons for my persistence here is that I was a very shy, no, super shy kid from as early as I can remember. As I said earlier, I used to hide under my mother's skirt as often as I could. I'm thankful she didn't fart much, not that I can remember. Was I born shy? Did it start in the womb? Was it past-life karma? Were the first five years of my life so traumatic that I couldn't face the world anymore? I wouldn't be harping on this so much if it hadn't played such a crucial role in my life (it still does).

Some of the reasons for shyness are a fear of being ridiculed, being afraid of what others think, and a lack of self-confidence. Research tells me that there is no known reason for shyness, but possible causes may be in the genes, lack of bonding to parents, or being criticised or teased, or any of the three combined. I can only surmise that the severity of my shyness may have been caused by all three of these possibilities. I was the seventh of eight children, which could have created the lack of bonding, and with five older brothers vying for attention, I may have copped a bit of criticism and bullying. Why don't we play the victim a little further and say it was in the genes as well? Both my parents were quiet in nature and kept to themselves. They were each other's best and only friend. With eight children, I guess they didn't have time for anyone else.

This is that vital part of the story that will tell us who we were and confirm why we were who we were. Did you get that? Literary experts would probably pull that sentence to bits, but they're pains in the butt. We simple folk will understand everything I say. I would like to analyse it a little further and add that although shyness can affect us as small children, we sometimes don't know any different and may not think we have any serious issues. It's just part of being a kid, so we cope with it. If the shyness persists, which it does in most cases, it can have major effects on the social skills of the child whilst growing up and well into adulthood.

There is no need for me to research this, as I can speak from experience. Chronic shyness, if I can use that term, is my field of expertise. I don't recall having any social skills as a child. In fact, I never knew what they were and had not properly acquired them till my late twenties (or is that thirties, maybe forties?). I went into business for myself in my late twenties, which forced me to relate to people a lot more. My social skills had to improve, as my livelihood demanded it. I was a skilled craftsman but a lousy communicator.

I got by, though, because of people's kindness, patience, and understanding, and I've always been appreciative of that. And not only that, all throughout history, it has been documented that most creative genius have lacked social skills. The fact that I can sit here and write a book, with confidence, albeit one finger at a time, about who I was, who I am, and who I'm going to be, which will sell millions and will save the world, is testimony to what can be achieved by one who has been handicapped by a chronic dose of lackness.

I just added that word to the Microsoft dictionary. I've found that it is okay to make up words. The English language is full of new words that have been made up over the years. The trick is to make it obvious what it means because you won't find it in the Oxford or Chambers, or any of those other toffy-nosed publications.

Where was I? Oh, yes. That could also be a dose of chronic lackness, a lack of self-belief, lack of self-confidence, being self-conscious, being self-effacing, having low self-esteem, and of course feeling unworthy. One of our greatest challenges is to always feel worthy.

So we've covered from birth to age five; well, actually, it's from ejaculation to pronunciation, and if we had any opportunities to save the world during this time, we certainly didn't take advantage of them. I'm still thinking indigo, though.

Chapter 3

There's no going back now, even if I wanted to. The womb is way out of bounds, and I'm at that point of no return, although in my later years, I become fascinated with the thereabouts of that part of a woman's anatomy.

There weren't any such thoughts at five years old. In fact, girls were as foreign to me as the structure of school, and both were the enemy. My only recollection of that very first day at school was sitting under a big gum tree at lunchtime and sobbing my eyes out. I was yearning for my mother, who had never left me anywhere for this length of time before. One of my older brothers came up and asked me what was wrong.

I sobbed to him, "I wanna go home."

He told me that it will be alright, and to go and play with the other kids. I don't remember much more than that, except that I was in a foreign place and didn't want to be there.

Very early on in the year, our teacher announced that we were going to have a debate. That's cool; a couple of kids had to address the class, one arguing that the pin was more useful than the needle, and the other, vice versa. To my horror, the teacher selected me to start the debate, for the pin. What was she thinking? Why did she choose me? I hadn't mumbled a word all year, and now I had to stand up, walk out to the front of the class with everyone staring at me, and talk about something I knew nothing about. Did I not tell you how shy I was?

I did not know that a public speaking course was a prerequisite to starting grade one. Nobody gave me warning, ever, that I was going to be made a fool of, humiliated, shamed, embarrassed, and scarred for life by a prissy, uninformed, ignorant grade one teacher, who obviously didn't have children of her own.

I stood there trembling with fear for what seemed like an eternity, and then I finally mumbled, "Ummmm," and then froze. I couldn't have said anything else even if I knew what I was talking about. The teacher finally told me, in disgust, to sit down.

If there was ever any doubt that I didn't exist on this planet or if I wasn't sure I was alive or not, I certainly knew then, and there was nowhere to hide. The security that I felt hanging onto my mother's skirt, and the safe feeling I had, just knowing she was around, had deserted me. I felt abandoned amongst a maze of alien predators that were eating me alive. (That is so dramatic. Hey! I'm trying to make a point here, and it's all part of the plan; it feels good to express the suppressed.)

Little Jimmy Digne was now the classroom dunce, the boy who couldn't tell the difference between a pin and a needle. I had to face these kids in the playground, some on the way home from school, and others on weekends, for the rest of the year. I do not recall ever having a friend in grade one. I thought they all hated me, and I resented them for it, but that was only because I thought I was useless and unlikable.

The crazy thing about all this is that by the time school finished that day, all those kids probably forgot the whole thing, with most of them feeling relieved that they hadn't been chosen for the debate. The teacher probably forgot all about it ten minutes after the event. Everybody has their own stuff to deal with. I was to carry this one with me for another forty-five years.

I'd like to touch on the resilience of a child. Even though the previous event was somewhat traumatic for me, I had to find ways to overcome it and move on. There is too much going on in the lives of kids for them to mope around all day. The trauma of the event was suppressed, as was the resentment I had for myself. What I thought the other kids thought of me was put aside, so that I was able to cope with school life with them in it. Therefore, there was no reason to think that they were against me, unless of course they criticised, ridiculed, or teased me. Then that would just be a reminder that I still resented myself.

The subconscious mind is very clever and very powerful. It's as if it spends all its time building up an arsenal of weapons, just to make our life miserable. For some reason, it doesn't want us to like ourselves or to think that we're any good. The thing to remember, though, is that it, our mind, belongs to us, and if we become aware of what we are doing to ourselves, then all we have to do is change our minds. In fact, if we change our minds, we change the world, and if we want to save the world, we have to cultivate our minds. That sounds a bit Buddhist to me. We might elaborate on that later on.

Of course, the needle and pin incident wasn't the only fear-riddled event in my childhood, but it was like a beginner's class into the insights of the crazy world we live in. It was the cementing of the foundations for the structure of my life. It was preparation for my adventures into the cruel unknown, and the beginning of the construction of an elaborate defence mechanism, but of course, I didn't know that at the time. The worst thing was this incredible shyness I had to contend with, and I was still wetting the bed every night, as well, and that didn't stop until I was twenty years old (and no, that's not a misprint).

I spent two years at this particular primary school, and I remember the headmaster's surname being abbreviated to "Scat." So obviously he got called Scat the rat. I didn't think he was that bad a headmaster, and I never copped his wrath. Oh, except the one time I got a gentle little warning. Her name was Toni, and I teased her all the way to school one morning. Little boys do that when they like a girl, but she didn't see it that way. My social skills had not developed at that stage, and what I really wanted to do was marry her. I swear, sometimes I think I arrived on this planet at the wrong time.

It was the only school where I didn't get the strap or the cane, or what we used to call the cuts. I would've been too young to receive that sort of punishment, anyway. I was always trying to be good, and I swear it was never my fault whenever I got into trouble.

We had moved to a different house at the beginning of grade two, and even though Dad was still working on a farm, this home was closer to suburbia. This was where he bought his first car, a 1940 black Oldsmobile, with suicide doors, running boards, and whitewall tyres. It was plenty big enough for eight kids and two adults, and we all loved riding in that car. We must have looked like the mini Mafia. I can remember the many times when we had to crank it to get it going, and even getting my toes run over once, whilst playing the fool. Love that car.

As far as I can remember, this was a good year, not the tyres, the year; it was 1960. Dad was working for a guy who owned a small crop farm, and he had a farm horse that we kept in our big back yard. The Clydesdale, named Farmer, was used to pull the plough when preparing the ground for planting. Farmer only reacted to two commands: giddup and woah, and if he wasn't in the mood, he didn't take any notice of either. To plough a field would take a lot of coercing some days, and a little bit of cursing.

Dad and my eldest brothers also built a cricket pitch with chicken wire around three sides, so my older brothers could hone their skills. Howzat! He'd go out into the bush and gather the soil from the ants' nests, which was like clay, and spread it on the ground about two inches deep, scrape it level, water it lightly, and then roll it until the surface was very smooth and hard. Dad was very industrious and great at improvising. The scraper was made out of an old wheel rim, weighed down with a couple of bricks and dragged along with a piece of wire attached. The roller was a twenty-gallon drum filled with concrete with a rod through the middle as an axle so as to attach a handle. The impact of the cricket ball would leave an indent in the surface of the pitch, so the process of scraping, watering, and rolling would have to be done daily by one of my older brothers. I was too young to join in when they played but was always hovering around, waiting to get my hands on a stray ball.

One of the fondest memories of living at this particular place was the bonfire that Dad and the older ones had built for the neighbourhood on Guy Fawkes Night, November 5. It was the first bonfire I had ever seen and was set up in a clearing at the back of the property. All the neighbours had supplied a lot of rubbish, and it took weeks to pile up a pyramid of combustible materials about twelve feet high. It was a fun night, even though I was only allowed to play with the sparklers. There were all sorts of crackers and fireworks, with double bangers, penny bangers, rockets, jumping jacks, Catherine wheels, and golden rain. The rockets had to be supervised by the adults, who were having just as much fun as the kids.

I had no idea at the time why we celebrated what we used to call cracker night, or that Guy Fawkes was even a person. The story goes that in the year 1605, a group of men conspired to kill King James I by blowing up Parliament House in London. After a tip, Guy Fawkes was arrested on the fifth of November that year while he was preparing the explosives for detonation in the cellar under Parliament House. It is said that he may be the only man who's ever entered Parliament with honest intentions.

Not long before we left this house, I managed to sneak out with an older brother, and we crossed the road to climb down a steep embankment covered with scrub and tall gum trees all around. We didn't get very far before we came across a huge mass of water. I remember thinking, *Wow, where did this come from?* I'd never been exposed to anything like it in my short life so far, and so close to home. It felt like I had stepped into another world, a very beautiful world, and my perception of my existing world had changed, albeit ever so slightly; after all, I was only seven years old.

It just happened to be Townsend Bay, part of the South Pacific Ocean. We snuck back home, and I was still feeling overawed by such a great mass of water and very excited by my adventure, but couldn't share it with Mum, or we would have got into trouble.

She did ask later on if we had been across the road. We had to tell her the truth because she already knew. One of the others had obviously dobbed us in. She just said that we weren't allowed over there and not to do it again. My mother knew what was out there, and it was her fear of us drowning that kept us from experiencing something special. Sometimes, I think her obsession with protecting us was a kind of deprivation. I did go through a stage in later years of resenting her, but as a youngster, she was my world.

Chapter 4

Mum and Dad had this knack that whenever we moved from one house to another, it was around the end of year school holidays, and Christmastime 1961 was no different. The good thing about being poor was that there was never much stuff to move.

There were a lot of things very different about this move. One thing was that I was to start grade three at a new school. I was also a year older, and that seemed to make a lot of difference; hence, I felt more excitement. The house was a little bigger this time around and had a lot more land, ten acres, in fact. There was a huge shed opposite the house, about ten steps away, to be precise, and it was made of corrugated iron, painted red. At the corner of the shed just outside the front door grew a rose of Sharon. It was a tall spindly plant, and its flowers would first bloom as white in colour then turn pink and finally red before they died and dropped off. It was fascinating to watch as the tree was adorned with three different coloured flowers at the one time. There were also mango, custard apple, and mandarin trees growing nearby, but the rose of Sharon was my and my mother's favourite.

The property was mostly farmland, and it was the first time that Dad was able to share farm on his own, which meant that he would be his own boss. He could grow anything that he wanted and work the farm his way. We lived in the front corner of the property, while the owner, Mr Kerrigan, had a big house at the end of the long driveway, about three hundred yards away. The Kerrigans' house overlooked Townsend Bay and the many islands therein. He'd always said that having seen many places all over the world, none were as beautiful as this. I grew to agree. Why do tears well in my eyes every time I read that?

The smell of the rich red farming soil and the sea air were no different from whence we came, and it didn't take long to settle into this new abode. There were only four bedrooms, of which Mum and Dad had one and my sister had another. The math tells you that there were two bedrooms for the remaining seven children. The four youngest had two double bunks in one room, and the older three had single beds in the remaining. There was some serious coordination happening in that household, which only had one bathroom and one toilet, which was an outhouse fifteen yards away from the house. There was no hot water, so no one ever showered, but everyone always had their daily bath. The water was heated up using two old washing machines and bucketed up from the laundry down in the shed.

Not long after we moved in, Dad and Mum got their first-ever television. I think they were more excited than us kids. I can still remember coming home from school every arvo and watching shows like *Rawhide*, *Gunsmoke*, *The Rifleman*, *The Texas Rangers*, *Paladin*, *Bat Masterson*, and many others. There was a game we used to play at school where you could name a day and a time, and the first kid to say which show was on at that time got to have a turn. I knew every show that was on in every time slot for the whole week, all seven days, and so did most of the other kids. Consequently, it was a fast game.

Dad also built the customary cricket pitch, which was behind the outhouse. It was three pitches wide, which meant we didn't have to prepare it as much, as we could rotate from one to the other. My eldest brother still complains about how he ruined his car gathering the ant's nest from the bush and loading it in his boot to bring home. I can't help thinking, that that must have been a lot of boot loads.

I just had a book load of memories come flooding my way, and I don't have enough time to write a book on all my childhood memories. I'm still conscious of us saving the world with this one, so I don't think too many of my childhood experiences will help, unless of course it helps you to remember a lot of yours. If you stop for a while and reflect on your own childhood, particularly those really happy moments and then some not-so-happy experiences, you can start to realise a little bit about who you are, especially if you go deeper into the emotions that you felt at the time. You may even start remembering feelings that you have suppressed all your life.

I often smile while I write, as I remember some of the fun times, and then there have been moments when my chest aches and tears well in my eyes and roll down my cheek. I have to sit farther from the keyboard so that it doesn't get wet, which makes it hard to type sometimes, as I tend to want to go faster to get it all off my chest.

Lots of kids have had awful things happen to them, like a broken arm or leg, being hit by a car, being in a car crash, or being physically or sexually abused. Many have had parents who fought all the time, or parents who were alcoholics or drug addicts, or parents dying or deserting them. This can be a huge setback for kids growing up, particularly if they suppress the memories and the emotions around the event.

The build-up of their fear, both conscious and subconscious, will breed anger, resentment, and other negative emotions. We grownups call it baggage, which of course not only runs our lives, but can ruin our lives, if we're not aware of its presence. In fact, even when we are aware of the baggage, we feel helpless at preventing it from influencing our daily habits.

My parents never fought, or if they did, they didn't do it in front of their children. They would always hug and kiss in front of us, though, and you have no idea what a valuable lesson that was for us. I was a sensitive child, and their display of affection for each other was a great strength for me. There was a lot of chaos and madness, screaming and fighting amongst us kids at times, so it was good to experience some love and peace around dinner time. I still didn't like eating some vegies though, especially cabbage. Yuk.

I must admit, though, that Dad was very strict; he was like an aloof ogre to me. I think I spent most of my childhood in fear of him. I'm not saying that he did anything that made me frightened of him. I think it was because I was very shy and very sensitive, and he never had time for me because of his long hours at work. There were seven boys who needed pulling into line occasionally, as well, so no time for individual sensitees (added to dictionary).

Let's get back to the farm, which it was affectionately called; there are still lots of things I remember about it. I want to rattle off a few relevant things of interest, so that if I mention them later on, you won't be saying I didn't tell you about them. Work with me here, people. I'm still building the structure of our lives, without a plan or instructions. Do you remember the television show *The Greatest American Hero*? He knew he had powers that would save the world, but he lost the instruction manual. Get my drift?

There was a small dam in the other front corner of the property, which was surrounded by bush, with a narrow track leading down to it. A pump by the dam was used to draw water for irrigation. There was also a larger pump in the middle of the farm, which drew water from a bore and pumped it into the dam. The house was a fibro shack with a tin roof and sat on two-foot-high stumps. The outside was painted green, and the inside was only sheeted on one side of the framework, also with fibro, and unpainted. The hardwood frame being exposed allowed us to use the nogging for shelves. At a certain time of the year, there were plagues of mosquitos, and other times, we endured hordes of sandflies.

The property was bordered on three sides by mangroves, with one side being swampland. I loved it. It was also hard to get a good night's sleep sometimes, with either one of my brothers snoring, being eaten by mosquitos, the noisy bore pump, nightmares, or simply wetting the bed. The sandflies seemed to disappear when the sun went down, but not the mosquitos.

The eldest three bros were going to high school, and us other five went to the local primary school, which was within walking distance. In fact, every primary school we went to was in walking distance. It was a little farther this time; I don't know how my little brother coped with the distance, as he was starting grade one. He was probably a little more excited than me about going to school in grade one. He was not the shy type and probably happy to get out of home. It didn't seem such a big deal for me, either; maybe because I had a little brother to watch over and was now aware that my older brothers would protect me. My sister, well, that's another story. I might discuss her later.

One of the things I remember about this school was the free milk we would get every morning before class. They were small bottles, about one third of a pint, and some kids would bring flavouring to mix with it. Sometimes, the milk was warm, especially in summer, as it sat in the sun for a couple of hours before we got to it. I really enjoyed it, though, because of the long walk to school, I suppose.

In the early part of that year, I was struggling to come to terms with my sister Sarah and how embarrassing she was. The other kids kept asking me if she was my sister and what was wrong with her. I always reluctantly said yes and explained that she was born like that. I think the frustration showed one day, and my mother sat me down for a talk.

She said, "I want you to try to understand that Sarah is not like other kids. She was born with Down syndrome and has an intellectual disability, which means she is a lot slower in the head than you boys. You have to try and be patient with her."

It's not the news I wanted to hear but I already knew that there was something wrong with her, but that's the first time it had been discussed.

"Why didn't you call her Sarah Semper Digne?" I asked my mother.

She gave me a dirty look and sent me out to play.

I got to make many friends over the next few years, but I never really let anyone get too close to me, you know, the shyness, the bed-wetting, being self-conscious, and I think at times I was a little embarrassed about our house. I could never stay over at anyone's place or have anybody over, either. There was no room at our place, anyway.

There was an incident in grade five, as well, when I was too shy to ask the teacher if I could go to the toilet. I usually went just before class but must have forgotten this time. I tried to wait for the next recess but couldn't hang on any longer and finally had to ask the teacher. He was in a bad mood and abruptly said no. A few minutes later, I had peed everywhere, and it was running all over the floor. A couple of the kids called out that I'd wet my pants.

The teacher looked in horror and said, "Oh, my God, he's wet his pants."

I remember thinking, *What did you expect?* I cannot recall and have never been able to remember what happened next. I think it's one of those situations that get suppressed so deep that you never have to deal with it again. No one else mentioned it again, and I didn't hold it against the teacher. It was really my stupid shyness that caused the problem.

I went into my shell a bit after that and started to spend a lot more time on my own, especially on weekends. This was around the same time that I started hearing this strange voice, more like a whisper, like somebody trying to communicate with me. It was a soft voice and very soothing. I never felt threatened in any way; it felt like I was just talking to myself, except that I wasn't opening my mouth. It only happened when I was on my own, and I was starting to spend a lot of time that way. I was feeling very relaxed in my own company. I started to explore the nearby mangrove swamp and surrounding bushland. In fact, I spent most of my weekends there when I wasn't playing any sport.

The more time exploring this wilderness of beauty, the more I got to speak to (or should I say, listen to) the whisper, as I now called it. He would say things like, be who you are, and don't try to be someone you're not. The only thing I knew about myself was that I was very shy and had a stupid name.

"What's in a name?" he'd say.

Oh, great; now I'm giving him quotation marks.

"You become what you will, so will well." I knew what he meant with that one. It's not that what he always said made total sense to me; it was more that it kept me in a good state of mind. It would relieve a lot of the fear and stress. In fact, it would allow me to forget there was another world out there.

In class that same year, I remember tying an eraser to a piece of string and using it to hypnotise a classmate. This guy went into a trance very quickly, and I got a bit of a surprise. I must say, though, that this particular fellow looked like he was in a trance all the time. I think that's why he went under so easily. It was during class, and I was just messing around with him. It was an amazing experience at the time, especially when the other kids finally realised that it wasn't a joke.

The teacher started to wonder what the commotion was all about, and when we informed him, he told us not to be ridiculous. Just as I was about to bring him back, some kid from behind belted him in the back and woke him up. I told the kid not to be so stupid. The trancee (added to dictionary) was very dazed and wasn't impressed with being belted in the back. He recovered fairly quickly, though, and didn't remember a thing.

The 1960s was full of fads, with the hula hoop, yoyos, hopscotch, marbles, cap guns and cowboy outfits, and many new board games, not to mention turtlenecks, the Twist, and miniskirts. Oops, too young for that. Marbles and yoyos was the way to go for me, with the occasional hopscotch with the girls, but they were always too good for us guys, so we mainly stuck to the marbles. There were fierce battles going on under the big Moreton Bay fig tree in the schoolyard, with cat's eyes, tom bowlers, the steely, and stonkers (can't believe stonkers wasn't in the dictionary; is now). There was even this girl, Jill Reed, who walked around with a pouch full of marbles, always looking for a game. At first, we thought she would be easy pickings, but when she started to win our marbles and got a lot of joy out of it, we had to lift our game. She was a real tomboy and loved playing marbles with the boys. Some days, you won, and some days, you lost. They worked well in a slingshot too.

Another terrible experience for me was when I lined up, ready to race at an interschool sports carnival. You have to know the preparation that went into this, with Mum making the shorts, T-shirt, and the ribbon that we had to wear as a sash. I was really excited about being in the school team. As I was standing in line, a teacher came along doing head counts and then asked me what I was doing there. I wasn't on his list of participants, so I had to sit out of the carnival.

I was shattered but didn't want to show it, as I was also embarrassed, and it wasn't like I could just sit down where I was. I had to walk through a crowd of kids all lined up ready for the carnival. I went and sat behind an old gum tree for a while, picking up pebbles and throwing them at a nearby fence post. I didn't cry: I just thought of the whisper and then got up to join the other nonparticipants from our school, who were all cheering the runners on. Mum never found out; I just told her that I didn't do very well, but I did my best. It wasn't a lie; besides, the whisper helped me with that line. Mum always liked it when we'd say we did our best.

As I reflect back over my primary school years (which, by the way, I've never done before), I feel appreciation for the learning I gained and the teaching I received. But nothing was as important or more valuable than the relationships I experienced with all the kids and the schoolteachers. The people around us, particularly when we're children, help to shape who we are just by them being who they are, even if no one actually knows who they are. Things can only get better.

I never knew who I really was as a kid. I was lost and constantly trying to prove myself to others. This, of course, as I now realise, was a lack of self-worth. I was at my best when I was on my own, exploring the nature that surrounded our home. I couldn't maintain that peace and calm within society. I had a lot of anger and frustration that I seemed to vent at the drop of a hat. I felt synthetic and false, and it seemed like my surroundings were influencing who I was. My experiences, feelings, and emotions were dictating who I was becoming, and I didn't like that. I didn't want to resent myself, or lack confidence, or be shy. I didn't want to wet the bed anymore, either. I was starting to suffer from migraine headaches, and I'd had the measles, mumps, and chickenpox, and spent a month at home under quarantine for suspected hepatitis. I caught every cold and flu that was going around, every year. But you know, I just kept fronting up, as if it was all just part of being a kid, being human, being alive. I guess, too, that everything you are about to face during the day has got to feel better than getting out of a wet bed that morning.

I can't emphasise enough how much of a role the whisper played in supporting me through the tough times. He always reminded me that there was still a lot of life ahead and plenty of living to do, and to deal with things the best way I knew how at the time, and that as I got older, I'd find better ways of dealing with them.

"Your experiences are just that, experiences; they are not who you are," he would say.

I don't know about you people, but I think we're heading in the right direction here. We have to go back and find out who we were, to find out why we are. It doesn't matter if we lived a colourful, catastrophic, simple, or sordid childhood; the fact remains that those influences have made us who we are, and if that's the case, then we are false. So in reality, it's not a matter of finding out who we were, but who we were not. If we can come from a solid foundation built on the truth of who we are instead of a false impression, then the structure, which is our life, will stand firm and resolute in the fierce battle to save the world (just in case you forgot what we're here for).

My last year of primary school finished on a pretty good note. Although I copped the strap across the hand a couple of times early on, the year panned out okay. We did basket weaving, which I really loved. I was always good with my hands, and I think I inherited my improvisational skills from my father. A lot of my spare time at home was spent working on pushbikes and building crab pots, slingshots, crossbows, birdcages, and bird traps. I also built a raft by wiring together a number of twenty-gallon diesel drums and covering them with timber planks. I had to attach some homemade axles to put a couple of pushbike wheels on it. It was a real spectacle wheeling that thing down the road and into the water. It floated, and it worked well, of course.

The final term of grade seven had arrived, and although the daunting expectation of high school was always in the back of my mind, I stayed focused on finishing primary school with good marks. I was never the brightest student but was always above average. I could have done a lot better if I studied more. But studying never appealed to me, so I didn't do it very often. I never thought that school marks were a measure of somebody's intelligence, only their intellect. Some of the kids who were getting high marks used to do some dumb things, let me tell you. I had a friend, Brett Jones, the smartest boy in the class. One Xmas, his parents had invited me to spend two weeks on holiday with them up the coast. He was an only child, adopted, and I was the only kid who related to him at that time. Mum told me that it would be alright, as she'd spoken to Mrs Jones about my bed-wetting. I think Mum was glad to get me out of the way for a while too.

Whilst on holiday, I got a first-hand observation of an intellectual spoilt brat. He went to cross a road one day, walking out from between two cars. He didn't look either way, but fortunately I did, and I had to reach out and pull him back from an oncoming car. If I hadn't done that, he would be dead, no doubt.

Now, not only was I his best friend for life, but, "Hey Mum, James saved my life today" (not the most intelligent thing to tell your mother).

The worst part of the holiday was when Mrs Jones woke up one morning feeling very sick. Mr Jones informed me that I had to change my own bed and wash my wet sheets and pyjamas. I'd never done that before, and if I didn't appreciate my mother before, I did now.

I nearly drowned in the surf that holiday too, but that's another story, and there was a day visit by Brett's cousin, who peeled the skin off my nose with his knuckles, but that's another story too.

"Did you get a touch of the sun, James?" Mrs Jones asked. "Your nose is peeling."

I wanted to beat the crap out of that kid, but I was such a skinny little runt, and the situation did call for diplomacy. All these crazy things happening to me all the time. I just wanted some peace and calm in my life and for everyone to be like me. That wasn't too much to ask.

With subsequent visits to Brett's house in the remainder of the school holidays, I was starting to understand why he didn't have any other friends and the only one he did have was about to call it quits. He was an obnoxious pain in the butt who always got his own way. And get this: He scored 98 per cent in his final end-of-year exam. And get this: He was so upset that he didn't get 100 per cent, he started to cry. I wonder where that pressure came from.

With only a week or so of school to go, I was sitting towards the back of the classroom when a strange feeling came over me.

I turned to the girl behind and said to her, "I love you." I think the whisper was playing games with me. This was very strange for such a shy kid, and I couldn't control myself. I said it again: "I love you."

Her name was Susan Rhodes, and although I liked her, I never had a lot to do with her. She wasn't like a girlfriend, and I certainly wasn't in love with her. I was feeling an incredible peace and found myself in a zone of uninhibited bliss. I believe I was expressing who I was, and I definitely felt the presence of the whisper, this reverent whisper that seemed very much a part of me.

I turned to her again and repeated, "I love you. I love you. I love you. I love you. I love you. I love you. I love you. I love you. I love you."

The other girls around were astounded and probably jealous. They giggled and kept telling me to shush. Susan started to get a little embarrassed, but I could tell that she enjoyed the attention. I told her outside school later that I was sorry and didn't know why I had done that. She was okay with that. Maybe she was my wife in a past life, or I was meant to marry her in this one; another case of bad timing.

I doubt whether there would be too many twelve-year-old boys who would ever do something like that. I often think what an amazing experience it was. Imagine if we could go to a peaceful place like that at will. Imagine if everyone could have that incredible feeling, and all at the same time, over a longer period of time. Imagine.

It was a great way to finish primary school, and now for six weeks holiday before high school. I was thankful that I wasn't invited away with anyone, not that I was close to anyone anymore, anyway. Don't make me change that line. I like it. I think I would have refused to go if I was asked. I had some serious exploring to do, and I loved my pushbike as well.

I would spend hours pulling my bike to bits, changing wheels and tyres, refitting ball bearings in the axles, patching tubes, fixing chains, adjusting brakes. I had spare bike parts everywhere, and a section of the big shed became my workshop. I also pinched some of Dad's chicken wire to build a couple of crab pots. There was a large creek a couple of miles through the bush that I used to frequent quite often. I would get to the creek at low tide, tie the pots to the mangrove tree roots at the waterline, and come back at the next low tide. I used raw meat I would fetch from the butcher at the nearest shops. These shops were a fair hike, so I'd always ride my pushy. There would always be a mud crab or two, and I'd always throw the females back. Dad never minded me pinching the wire because he just loved to eat mud crab, and so did I. I loved catching them for him too.

My relationship with Dad wasn't always rosy, though, and he didn't hesitate to give us the strap if we played up. Sarah complained to Dad one day that my little brother and I were calling her a spastic. We would get frustrated with her sometimes, and that was the only word we could think of. We fiercely denied it, so Dad couldn't do anything about it. However, the next time I called her a spastic in frustration, Dad happened to hear me.

He said, "I've been waiting to hear you say that," and dragged me by the arm over to the back door where the strap was hanging and proceeded to belt me.

I was screaming even before we got to the door. I'm not sure if the punishment fitted the crime, and I felt Dad overstepped my sense of fairness.

I spent most of that summer holiday exploring almost every inch of land that surrounded the farm. There was such a contrast of landscape that I never got bored, even walking through the mud and the mangroves. There were sandy sections that opened out into the bay and others that were surrounded by mangroves. There was a vast mud plain between the bush and the bay that was covered at high tide, and in some areas, I would sink almost to my knees. There was a track through the bush that weaved its way to the creek, and sometimes I'd ride my bike as fast as I could go, but most times, I enjoyed a slow stroll. It was truly a piece of paradise, and I believed that it all belonged to me. I felt a part of it, and I felt safe being there, and I felt the whisper walking with me (or should I say, hovering above me), everywhere I went. It was my world, with the supposed real world seemingly so far away.

I was beginning to understand the affinity that indigenous tribes of the world have with their land and why they treasured it so much. It was a feeling of belonging somewhere, belonging there, but never owning it. The transient and nomadic indigenous races must have had the most incredible feeling of freedom. The ability to move across vast areas of land whenever they felt the need would have given them a sense of gratitude for not just living somewhere, but living everywhere. I wondered, too, if they ever thought about saving the world, but I guess back then, everything they did was about saving the world. They just didn't know it. Or did they?

Chapter 5

High school was the pits. The third day in, I had a physical education period, and when I went to change back into my uniform, I could not do my tie up, or tie my shoelaces, either. The teacher begrudgingly helped me and a couple of others with our ties, and another student showed me how to tie my shoes. Consequently, when I got home that afternoon, I had Mum teach me how to do a tie up, and then I practised till I got it perfect. I'll be honest with you right now: I did not like wearing a hat, a tie, socks, shoes, and a uniform, and I never got used to it, either.

The grade eight teachers were very nurturing, as they obviously realised that the transition into high school could be difficult, but as time went on, they started to get a little more serious. It soon became obvious, and older students confirmed it, that they were looking for A, B, and C students to place into the grade nine structure. I was very conscientious and started off pretty good, as I wanted to do well at high school. I didn't mind maths and English, and did very well at them in the early stages. But the harsh reality of high school was to set in very quickly.

One morning, I was coming back from the science laboratory with my class. While walking down the stairs at the end of the building, a group of students from grade ten were coming up. One of them, whose nickname was Tank, grabbed me by the shoulders, dragged me towards him, and thrust his knee into my balls, saying, "Welcome to high school, little grade eighter," and then continued on his way.

I could hear them laughing all the way up the stairs. I took a couple more steps down before I buckled over with the most excruciating pain I'd ever experienced. I was thinking, why me; out of all the guys walking with me, why did he single me out? Was it because I was so little? Why would someone do that to another person? How could he do it with such vicious intent? I could never imagine doing that to another person. I was soon to learn that that's just the way it is at high school. It was nothing personal. He was just showing off to his mates. It may have even been a dare, and I was in the wrong place at the wrong time. Later, I'd often pass by him, and he wouldn't even notice me (although I made sure I never got that close).

The irony is that about a couple of weeks later, I was watching him and his mates practising high jump during lunch break. He made it over the bar, but he landed awkwardly and broke his wrist. He was screaming in pain, and I could feel his anguish. There was an opportunity for me to laugh or even say something like, "Serves you right," or "It couldn't have happened to a nicer bloke," or "That's the square up." Okay; those things did flash into my mind, but all I could do was feel for him. I remember wondering if there was something wrong with me. I felt no malice at all.

Settling into grade nine was fairly easy, a few different classmates, new teachers, a couple of fewer subjects, and some grade eighters if we felt the need to bully anyone. That was never my scene, unless of course they asked for it.

The best part of grades nine and ten were the woodworking, metalwork, and sports day. I didn't make it into the A group, but I was very happy as a B. My math teacher was an elderly lady, and she loved me because I was so good at them. She asked me one day if I was going on to be a teacher. She obviously believed that teachers were the be-all and end-all of everything. I very diplomatically replied that I'd never given it much thought but that I didn't think so. She said that I should consider it. The thought of being a schoolteacher was the furthest thing from my mind.

She asked one day if everyone had done their homework. I deliberately didn't do mine because I knew she would let me off, being her pet and all. I gave her some lame excuse, and she okayed it and let me off. Surprise. Surprise. The other kids objected because they were never let off. And this is where she let me down badly by saying, "James is an excellent student and doesn't need the extra work." I was beginning to wish I'd done my homework. The class riff-raff was after blood.

It wasn't even a couple of weeks when one of those riff-raff and I collided while trying to walk out the door at the same time. I gave him a friendly nudge, at which he reciprocated, and after a couple more minor pushes, the dukes went up. I slipped in three lefts, which connected harmlessly on his cheek, but forgot to block his right-hander, which connected with my nose. He was barracked on by his mates, who were mostly girls. It all came to a halt when blood started to drip from my nose, and I had to clean up before it went all over my uniform. I told him that if any teachers asked questions, I would tell them that I'd run into a door, and that was that. Mind you, I've seen teachers sit back and watch guys bash each other for a while before they cut in.

I turned fourteen halfway through that year and was starting to get tired of school, which in turn saw my grades drop. It was also the beginning of my growth spurt, and I felt myself changing, not just physically, but with my attitude towards everyone and everything. I felt it was time for me to toughen up, and if that meant rebelling and getting into a couple of fights, then so be it. High school was starting to become more about sticking up for myself, rather than getting an education.

I was being sexually molested at the time and was struggling to deal with it, as I always felt like it was my fault and there was no way anybody was to know about it. I'm not going into details with you, as the ramifications would be far reaching and much too painful. It is so difficult to explain or talk about something like that. Maybe if we don't talk about it, then it doesn't exist. I've spent a lot of time wondering why it is so devastating for the victims. Has society placed such a stigma to it that it is impossible to allow it into the light of day?

There was a lot of guilt, shame, and resentment building up, and it needed to be dealt with, so I suppressed it. The fact that I didn't think much of myself anyway probably made it a lot easier. I was a master at storing stuff away, and I knew I had another place I could go to when things got tough. The whisper was always there when I needed someone. In fact, he was the only one I ever related to. It was strange, really, how I knew if I could just get away occasionally and find some peace, he would always comfort me.

"Don't dwell on the past; it will cloud the present," he'd say.

"I just want to beat the crap out of someone," I'd tell him. I learnt early on that he would only be there when I was calm, and being in my piece of paradise would always bring me peace of mind.

I would like to pause for a moment, people, and reflect on a few things. This shouldn't take long. I don't know about you or if you are paralleling this story with your own childhood experiences, but I slipped into a state of depression for a couple of days and couldn't do much writing. I suffered from depression most of my adult life and was only able to overcome it when I was forty-nine years old, after I experienced a life-changing phenomenon that I will talk more about later on.

All through those years, I could never understand why I would get so depressed; a lot of the time, it came immediately after I was feeling happy and on top of the world. I actually had to control being happy so that I wouldn't get so low. I think it worked sometimes. Depression is a state of mind that can often be unbearable. The feeling of hopelessness and despair can be crippling; the dark cloud that never goes away leaves one in a hopeless situation. I often found myself languishing in this state of debilitation; the only cure was time. I must stress to you now that if you suffer from depression, then seek help, even if you don't believe you need it; seek it.

In recent times, when I've felt a little down, I bring myself to the present moment and look at the good and positive things in my life. I focus there for as long as I can, and if I start to lose focus, then I just keep coming back to now.

The amazing thing with this recent rare bout of depression is that I could see it for what it was. Because I've been writing about my traumatic childhood experiences, I got depressed as the memories and emotions around the events were stirred up. On the surface, these events seem insignificant to me now, and I believed that I had dealt with them on all levels of consciousness. I now realise that I have more work to do, albeit not too difficult. The realisation that the depression throughout my adult life was due to suppressed childhood feelings and emotions was very significant. If, in my subconscious mind, I had been building up regret, guilt, shame, resentment, and other nasty negatives, it would explain not only who I was but who I was becoming. Something I have learnt recently is that we unconsciously create situations in our lives so as to justify the negative emotions. If, for example, I was carrying a lot of guilt and shame, then it is a very real possibility that I attracted the sexual abuse into my life. This mind stuff is fascinating. Let's get back to the stories and see what else we can dig up.

If writing about the first eight years of school has caused a bout of depression, then the next eighteen months is going to send me into orbit. That may just be where we need to go to find out who we are, to get another perspective on things, so to speak. Stay with me on this because I'm starting to get a clearer picture of us. Besides, I have a few more stories to tell, as I'm sure you have, and I'm certain they've helped to shape our lives. It was an interesting age, and they were interesting years, 1968 and '69.

When I look back at that period of time, I can recall the chores that our parents used to get us kids to do. One of my older brothers was in Vietnam, and the other ones had either left home or outgrown the chore stage. Every morning before high school, my little brother and I had to either wash and dry the dishes or sweep and mop the floors. Sarah would help out as best she could, but she never liked to. Even after school, sometimes, we'd help out in the shed. If it was tomato season, and it had rained, we'd sit around and dry a thousand tomatoes or more, as they couldn't be packed while wet. In cucumber season, they had to be washed, as they'd be covered in red soil. As much as I thought the chores were a pain, I believe they were helping me to develop a good work ethic. You could not have convinced me of that at the time.

It wasn't always drudgery. There were the fun times with cabbage picking. All us kids would line up in the cabbage patch while Dad would cut them from the plant and hand it to one of us, and then it would get passed along the line until it was finally placed in a large crate. It was always fun, especially when Dad got farther and farther from the crate. He used to grow big cabbage, and they got heavy after a while. It was only when a couple would hit the ground that he ordered us onto a nearer crate.

I have to tell you about my brother Phil and the wayward tractor. Dad sent him on the tractor to pick up more empty tomato cases from the shed. On his way back, one of the cases fell off, so he jumped off to pick it up, with the tractor still moving, so the story goes. Suddenly, the tractor veered to the left. It ploughed (pardon the pun) through the bushes, went down the hill towards the dam, and finally came to rest in the thick shrub below. We had no idea what had happened, so it looked very strange when we could see him walking towards us with no tomato cases and no tractor.

One of the things I really hated doing was chores for the Kerrigans. We'd take turns in doing different things for them: collecting their empty milk bottles and returning them full the next day after the milkman had been, delivering their newspaper, weeding their garden, and any other menial task that Mum would want us to do for them. I even had to clean and polish their silverware on more than one occasion. Can you believe that? They had a dog that wanted to bite me all the time, but no one wanted to hear about it. It was always a cat-and-mouse game trying to get to their front door without the dog seeing me. It sunk its teeth into my rump one day, but fortunately, it didn't hurt much. They got rid of the dog not long after that, which came as such a relief. I felt like the fear-riddled sacrificial lamb that had won a battle, but the damage was done.

The Kerrigans were very good to Mum and Dad, and helped them through a lot of tough times when either a crop failed, or the drought hit, or even when a hailstorm wiped out a season's planting. I think they felt obliged to help the Kerrigans out anyway they could, and I felt a lot of that burden fell on me. Mum used to clean their house for them from time to time, and on one occasion, she asked me to help her out. They weren't home this day, and Mum was busily cleaning the main bedroom, when for some reason, I started opening and closing drawers to their big wardrobe. To my surprise, there was a handgun sitting on top of some shorts. I couldn't resist and just had to pick it up, as I'd never seen anything like it before, except in the western shows on television. There were a lot of gun tot'n' cowboys on the television, and most of the movies showing at the picture theatres were westerns.

Mum and I had our backs to each other, and she didn't notice that I'd picked the gun up and cocked it. Suddenly, I thought, *What do I do now?* There was an opportunity to point it out the window and pull the trigger to find out if it was loaded. I was concerned that the bullet might hit someone, if at all there were bullets in it. I made a snap decision to get this over and done with and face up to the consequences later. I pointed it at the front of the drawer from whence it came and pulled the trigger.

Well, cowboys, the damn thing was loaded, wasn't it? After a frightening bang, I heard a short sharp squeal from my mother, and I turned to see the horror on her face as she held her hands against her heart.

"Christ, Jimmy, you could have killed me," she said, quivering. She sat on the bed for ages with this look of disbelief on her face.

I put the gun back in the drawer and closed it, and said, "I knew what I was doing. You weren't going to be harmed."

My mother was in shock for the rest of the day. She was wondering how this was going to be explained to Mr Kerrigan as well. I eventually had to face Mr Kerrigan on my own, in his office. He gave me a good dressing down but admitted later that he probably shouldn't have a loaded gun in the house.

It wasn't the only terrifying thing I did. One day, I borrowed my little brother's magnifying glass, without asking him. I wanted to experiment with it, as I'd never had one before. I'd always be taking his stuff without his permission, and it really annoyed him. It was in the summer and a very hot day. I held it between the sun and my arm to see how hot my arm would get. Ouch! It got very hot very quickly.

I headed down to the end of the street, not with any plans, but just wanting to be on my own with my score. I walked into the bush a little bit, where I came across some very dry horse manure settled into the very dry grass. I never knew that horse manure was so combustible, so when I tried my trick with the magnifying glass, it exploded into flame, and so did the grass and the bush. I had no time to try and put it out, so

I took off back home. It wasn't long before the cry went out: Fire! Bush fire!

Dad, the neighbour, and my older brothers all went off fighting the fire. Mum wouldn't let my little brother or I go. She said it was too dangerous. I heard our neighbour say that the damn kids could have started the fire. I remember wondering how he knew and feeling guilty at the same time.

I was a bit more pleased when I heard Dad say that the fire would do more good than harm. Fortunately, it was only the northeast edge of the property, and my beloved bushland to the west was spared. It was a valuable lesson on the dangers of fire, and of course, magnified glass.

I was just about at the age when I'd had enough of the haircuts that Dad used to give us. It was a short back and sides with a bit of a mop on top. I was seriously starting to rebel against them, and it was causing a rift between Dad and I. Many of the older guys at school were starting to grow their hair longer, and I liked the look of it. It was the middle of the hippie era, and I liked the fact that people were bucking the system. There will be more on that later.

My brother who had been in Vietnam for almost a year was due home around September of 1968. It must have been the longest time in my mother's life. She seemed to be worried the whole year, and it was very difficult to reassure a person whose son was fighting in a war. We were very relieved for her when we heard that he was on his way home. He had been drafted into the army against his will, and they had brainwashed him into becoming a fighting and killing machine. Fortunately, he didn't see any combat where he was stationed.

I had been at school that day and couldn't wait to get home. He was arriving on a boat, and my parents and eldest brother had gone into the city to pick him up. It was hours before they got home, and I was getting more and more excited by the minute. I heard the car pull up, so I waited near the clothesline beside the house. I could hear them walking up the side of the shed, and they sounded a little intoxicated. It's really hard to describe the feeling at that moment. He was eight years older than me, and I had a lot of respect for him. He was a very kind and gentle person with a very placid nature, and he always treated me well. His personality had changed a little, but that was the obvious influence of being in the army.

He came into view, and it was a feeling of relief that came over me. I suddenly realised that he was actually home. He spotted me standing there and approached me with a smile on his face, a bit shocked that I'd grown so much.

He said, "Wow, you've grown," and then I felt a punch to the side of my head, and the next one hit me on the cheek.

Someone pulled him away, and I just stood there in shock for a few seconds and then turned and walked away, with tears welling in my eyes. It wasn't what I expected, and in my state of mind, it certainly wasn't what I needed. The punches never really hurt, but I'd never felt so shattered in all my life. I'm forcing myself to write more about the incident, only because I feel it will be helpful to me and others. It doesn't seem a significant event now, but at the time, and for the next thirty-three years, it hung over me like a heavy load weighing me down.

I guess I was asking myself if that was all I was worth, not just to him, but to everyone. The fact that I was standing there waiting for him, to catch a glimpse of him after all that time, was my way of showing love for him. It's sad, really, because I never looked at him the same or loved him the same, which was to hurt me more than him.

The sixties was a great time, and the stuff that was happening in the world seemed to make my life more normal. The Vietnam War was the most significant event of the decade, and it was even more prevalent to our family for obvious reasons. Another older brother was called up but didn't go overseas, much to the relief of us all. The protests by the American kids were flashed across our television screen just about every night. I must admit I was dead set against war, even though I didn't understand that much about it at the time. It just didn't feel right or seem to make any sense. You can't save the world by waging war upon it.

America saw a lot of assassinations too, which sickened me. I was disgusted with the assassination of JFK ("Ask not what your country can do for you, but what you can do for your country. Some men see things as they are and ask why. I dream things that never were and ask why not"), his brother Robert Kennedy ("Our future may be beyond our vision, but it is not completely beyond our control"), Martin Luther King ("I have a dream, that one day this nation will rise up and live out the true meaning of its creed"), Malcolm X ("Who taught you to hate yourself from the top of your head to the soles of your feet"), and Medgar Evers ("Don't buy gas where you can't use the restroom").

I must admit, though, that the assassination of President Kennedy was the one that traumatised me the most. I think it must have been because I was at an impressionable age, and my innocence was relatively intact. I wonder at times how deeply the impact of the event affected me. We can suppress things so far that we don't realise how they are actually playing out in our world.

It was the decade of Bob Dylan, the Beatles, Elvis Presley, birth control, the Cold War, civil rights, LBJ, and Nixon. I found Timothy Leary very interesting: "Admit it. You aren't like them. You're not even close. You may occasionally dress yourself up as one of them; watch the same mindless television shows as they do, maybe eat the same fast foods sometimes. But it seems the more you try to fit in, the more you feel like an outsider, watching the 'normal people' as they go about their automatic existences. For every time you say club passwords like 'Have a nice day' and 'Weather's awful today, eh?', you yearn inside to say forbidden things like 'Tell me something that makes you cry' or 'What do you think déjà vu is for?' Face it; you even want to talk to that girl in the elevator. But what if that girl in the elevator (and the balding guy who walks past your cubicle at work) are thinking the same thing? Who knows what you might learn from taking a chance on a conversation with a stranger? Everyone carries a piece of the puzzle. Nobody comes into your life by mere coincidence. Do the unexpected. Find the others", as well as Woody Guthrie, Sonny and Cher, the Stones, Cream, *Easy Rider,* Barry McGuire's "Eve of Destruction," Hendrix, and Joplin. There were magic mushrooms, marijuana, Monterey and Woodstock, the moon landing, Manson, My Lai, and Lennon's "Lie In." There was *Hair,* hippies, the mini minor and miniskirts, love-ins, flower power, flares, bell-bottoms, polar necks, and tie-dye. Wow! No wonder I stayed sane.

It was also the realisation of the Age of Aquarius, which at the time meant absolutely nothing to me. The musical *Hair* created interest in the new age, and there is still debate whether we are really in the Age of Aquarius or not. My instincts tell me that we are.

My only experience with hippies was when a few decided to have a beach party on the edge of the farm one Saturday night. The rockers from the local township found out about it and rolled up for a crash and bash. We only found out what was going on when there were naked hippies running all over the property and passing by my bedroom window. They were being chased by the rockers. I didn't get to see much in the dark, but it was very exciting for a fourteen-year-old. The police ended up coming, and they were chasing the rockers because the hippies had rung for help.

I was so excited about the whole thing; I decided to write my English composition about it. I visited a couple of our neighbours to see if I could get more information and was amazed at how much they could tell me about the incident. They were all excited too, because not much happens in this vast neighbourhood. I put it all together on paper, and I was very pleased with it, so I took it to school the next day.

All the students were fascinated and wanted to hear all about it. When our English teacher collected all our compositions, the class wanted her to read mine because they felt it would be the most exciting. She started to read it to herself, and about halfway through, she stopped and told me how disgusting it was and I shouldn't write about such filth. Then she threw it at me and told me to get rid of it. The other kids tried to tell her that it was a true story, and that it should be okay. She was quite adamant and didn't want to discuss it any further. One can only assume that she had some sexual hang-ups at the time.

Do you ever have those moments when you wish you could go back in time, knowing what you know now? I now understand more than ever what the hippies were trying to do, even if they didn't know themselves. They were trying to break the shackles of ignorance and set our spirits free. It's strange how we saw the hippies as if they were another race of people or rejects from another planet. They were actually human beings just like you and me, and they were just making a statement. Things like, peace not war, love not hatred, freedom from social restrictions and the conformists of society.

It was a kind of self-expression and liberating themselves from the suit-and-tie fraternity. The word *hippie* actually means "one who is aware" and was not a name the hippies gave to themselves. The media at the time formed the terminology. Jerry Rubin, a social activist during the sixties, had a view on the hippies and was quoted as saying, "They mostly prefer to be stoned, but most of them want peace, and they want an end to this stuff." That could be the catchphrase for every generation of youth since. It's sad how we end up getting caught in the social pressures of the materialist, consumer culture.

After another fantastic summer in paradise, it was back to school, and I'd decided that grade ten would be my last year. I had no idea what was beyond that; maybe an apprenticeship in a trade would be best. There was always the option of helping Dad out on the farm, but at that stage, it seemed unlikely, as farming didn't appeal to me, and my relationship with my father was worsening.

Throughout my youth, I'd always loved playing sport, with tennis and cricket being my two favourites. I always liked to think that I was very talented at both; however, my lack of self-confidence and low self-esteem would always get in the way of my development. My shyness would not allow me to promote myself in any way. It would always be a source of great frustration, especially when I knew deep down that I was as capable as anyone. Are you people relating to this, or were you all obnoxious pricks who thought you were good at everything? I did warn you that I was starting to get an attitude.

A new guy started that year, a really good fella I befriended right from the start. His name was Steve Brown, and he had an older sister, Jean, who started grade eleven. She was a stunner and way out of my league, a bit snobby as well. Steve and I sat together in class the very first day and awkwardly introduced ourselves. I'd never done that before, and it felt strange. He commented that it seemed like a really nice school. I told him not to worry because I'd learnt to handle myself and to stick with me. It felt good to be able to offer support to a fellow student and to suddenly feel a little more secure in that environment.

Steve then said, "Oh, it's okay. I have a black belt in judo."

I replied, "Then you can take care of both of us."

After chatting for a while, I said to him, "It might be a good idea if you kept that black belt thing to yourself. There are a few guys in this school that would want to test you on it."

He understood what I meant and replied, "Okay."

I wasn't sure if he was joking or not about the black belt, so I asked him what he had learnt. He said something really strange to me, which I'd forgotten straight after he told me. I researched it (Guru Google) for us, because I remembered it being very profound.

He said, "When you seek it, you cannot find it. Your hand cannot reach it; nor does your mind exceed it. When you no longer seek it, it is always with you."

Shit, Steve; I only wanted you to show me an arm hold or something.

Steve was not your average guy, but I liked him, and I'm not sure whether he was influencing me or the other way around. We didn't always hang out together at school, but when we did, we'd talk about stuff that I'd never talk to anyone else about. I even told him about the whisper, and he seemed to understand. I mentioned his sister a couple of times, and I met her once, but she was always so vague and distant. She didn't seem to make friends easily, for someone so pretty. I knew what the older guys were like, as I'd seen them flirting with some of the young female teachers. I would have loved to have shown her my piece of paradise.

It was coming to the end of first term, and I was starting to wonder how I was going to get through the year. I was sitting in the first class of the morning one day when the teacher told me that I was wanted in the office. I had no idea why. It was my first visit to the office, so I walked up the stairs and along the veranda all the way to the end, passing the second-floor classrooms as I went.

There's been a lot of debate over the years about whether kids should be caned or not. Having been the recipient of that type of punishment this day, and remembering my thoughts about it at the time, I think I can offer some accurate insight into the subject.

On walking back to class from the headmaster's office via the water trough, where I was soothing my stinging fingers, I had time to reflect on what just happened. I thought what a total waste of time. The physical punishment did not fit the crime; in most cases, as in mine, I was just having fun and didn't even know I was doing anything wrong. For some reason, I was able to see the big picture, but most kids would have hated the headmaster for his actions and the prefect for dobbing him in. Resentment for both of them and the establishment would have grown over time, which would serve no purpose at all. I felt all these things but was able to let them go by the time I got back to class. I was never to commit that misdemeanour again, but I had to cut back on a lot of fun for fear of punishment (or make sure I never got caught).

My science teacher was a chubby fellow, and he began to gather pace as he was bounding towards me, with his face getting redder. I was starting to freak. All I did was show my excitement about getting a better grade on my exam this time. I could never understand and even wondered why I ever bothered with science. This teacher was not happy with my score, and when he reached me, he grabbed the front of my shirt and shook me ferociously until tears welled in my eyes.

I think the old girl maths teacher was boasting to the other teachers all the time about how she could get the best out in me, so why couldn't they? She may have loved me as a student, but she certainly wasn't doing me any favours by spreading those rumours about my intelligence.

My little brother had an indifferent attitude towards school. The bus stop was about three miles from home, and as we were walking out the driveway one morning, he decided to make a right turn. "That's the wrong way to the bus stop, mate," I said. "Where are you going?"

"I don't feel like school today," he replied and continued to head towards the bush; my bush.

Apart from being a little astonished by his brazenness, I was amazed by the trust he was putting in me. If I was to mention it to anyone at all, another student, another brother, a teacher, anyone, he would have got into a lot of trouble with Mum and Dad. He did it a few times, and I even joined him once, but it was too boring for me, sitting at the base of an old paperbark tree, with its huge branches hanging down to the ground keeping us hidden from view. The cigarettes we smoked were menthol as well, and after a while, they tasted terrible.

School was a bit more peaceful in grade ten, and I never felt that I had to keep looking over my shoulder. One morning, I had this amazing moment. I had to go to the toilet just before a class, and I found myself in there on my own. I'd just finished washing my hands when Baz Warner and two of his gorilla mates walked in. Baz was one of Tank's mates and without doubt the most feared bully in the whole school, and someone I had avoided for almost two and a half years. They had obviously seen me walk in and must have wanted to get to know me. I was expecting a beating.

He was surprisingly quite short in stature but always had two big guys by his side. But don't let that fool you, people; he could fight. I prepared myself for the worst and slowly backed up against the wall, as I didn't want to be grabbed from behind. Baz noticed my manoeuvre and walked to within two feet of me, flanked by his boys, and stared into my eyes. I kept still and stared back. He had a baby face and light blue eyes. His hair was a mousy colour, wavy, and almost reached his shoulders in length. I felt so at peace, like the time I kept telling Susan Rhodes I loved her.

I felt fearless and powerful, and I was ready to tear these three guys apart. I'm a madman, and Holden Caulfield would have been proud of me and all. Baz finally gave me a wry smile, which I reciprocated. He wasn't silly, and I knew he sensed a readiness in my calm demeanour. My earlier manoeuvre against the wall would have given him indication of that. I could tell that he was weighing up his options, his motives, and his risk.

I finally broke the ice when I said, "Go on; hit me."

He gave me another wry smile, nodded a couple of times, and then turned and slowly walked out, with his goons close behind.

I stood there for a few seconds, feeling very relieved. Referring to the whisper, I said, "I don't know if you had anything to do with that, but thank you anyway." I never mentioned the incident to anyone, not even Steve. I thought it best that what happens in the toilet stays in the toilet.

By the middle of year ten, most of my teachers were getting exasperated with me. They knew and I knew that I had the intelligence to do the work, but I just couldn't be bothered. There was too much psychological and emotional stuff going on, and schoolwork was too much to cope with. I was messing around in an English lesson one day when this book came crashing into my shoulder. I looked up and saw an irate Miss McGrath staring at me. I thought, *Here we go again; that damn old maths teacher's been in her ear too.*

Miss McGrath was very attractive, and I felt terrible because I liked her, and she was a good teacher, and before that moment, I thought we got on pretty well. She started to tell me, in a quivering but stern voice, that I was better than that, and if I applied myself a bit more, I could do very well.

Then she said, "Pass my book back, please."

Not long after that, she informed us that she was getting married and would be leaving school soon, and she looked very happy about it (getting married, I mean). On her final day, a lot of the students were queuing up to get her to sign their English books. I thought, *Why not?* I got in line, and when it was my turn, she looked up in surprise.

"Mr Digne," was all she said.

I replied, "So you're getting married, Miss McGrath. I thought you'd wait for me."

She smiled, signed my book, and said, "Good luck, James."

"Thank you, Miss McGrath," I replied.

Steve and I were starting to spend a bit more time together too, and he didn't seem to be as self-assured as I first thought. His sister, Jean, was still around, and don't worry, I was checking her out every chance I got. She was at least acknowledging that I existed, which was a plus. Maybe I'd marry her one day.

But my mind was soon to be taken off her when one day, this grade nine chick named Sue Banks started up a conversation with me. I'd never seen her at school before; she seemed to appear out of nowhere and sat beside me at our morning break.

She was petite, skinny, very pretty, and very forward. She had straight blonde hair which sat just above her shoulders. I was looking fairly cute at this stage, as my hair was getting a little long. The more my hair grew, the more my self-esteem grew. She didn't mess around and made it quite clear that she would like to indulge in sex. I think the whisper ran a mile that day, because I had no idea how to deal with the situation.

She must have been barely fourteen years old, and I wasn't even fifteen yet. I was just too shy for this, but I was not going to let her know that. Before things got too messy for me, a teacher suddenly appeared and told us to separate and not to fraternise at school. Maybe the whisper was there.

You wouldn't believe it, but my father had set aside that afternoon to cut my hair. Boy, didn't I protest, but to no avail; short, back, and sides, with a mop on top. The next day at school, I wouldn't go near Susan, even though she said that she liked my haircut. A guy in her class, who I knew, told me that she was a mole. I told him that I knew that and didn't care. I didn't even know exactly what a mole was, and because of my short hair and low self-esteem, I didn't pursue her anymore. I wish it had crossed my mind to get her phone number or find out where she lived, though. I just can't get the timing right with all these future wives.

It was a week before my fifteenth birthday, and things were getting a little crazy. I told Mum that I didn't think I could get through to the end of the year, but she encouraged me to continue the best I could and said that it was only another six months. She made it sound so easy. Steve was starting to annoy me a bit too. He seemed so immature and was always complaining about his old man and Jean, and what a bitch she was. I suggested that I visit him one weekend so I could get to know her a bit better, and you know, maybe get a gang together, and have some fun or something. That idea didn't go down too well.

"My old man would never allow that," Steve moaned.

The next day at school, I asked Steve to show me some judo moves but to go easy on me. We were messing around, throwing each other all over the place, when a teacher raced over to us. I thought we were in big trouble for sure, but he wanted to talk to Steve about Jean. She had broken down into tears and wouldn't tell anyone what was wrong. I went with Steve, and when we got there, she was screaming at everyone to leave her alone. I'm not saying that she was on drugs, but it was very weird to see someone act like that, and scary too. Steve tried to calm her down and put his arm around her. Their mother arrived soon after and took her to the doctor's. I asked Steve what was wrong with her and said that I'd never seen anyone behave like that.

He just shrugged his shoulders and said, "That's Jean."

When I got home, I told Mum what had happened and asked if it would be alright to invite my friend Steve over on the weekend. She said it was okay, but if he was staying overnight, to consider my social issue. I knew what she meant.

She also said, "This girl might be pregnant, you know."

I thought about that for a moment but couldn't comprehend it, so I let it go. I did wonder about the ramifications, though, knowing what I'd heard about Steve's father.

The next day, I couldn't wait to get to school so I could invite Steve over for the weekend. I went looking for him, but he wasn't anywhere to be found. I asked a couple of our classmates if they had seen him, but they hadn't. He never takes days off, so I thought it strange. It was the last lesson before lunch when the teacher announced that Steve's sister had overdosed the night before and taken her own life.

I couldn't comprehend what I'd just heard but felt I had to deal with it right then and there, so I cried, and cried, and cried. I didn't even know why I was crying. Maybe I … oh, forget it. I know why I'm crying now.

I went to school the next day, hoping to see Steve, but he didn't show up. When I got home that afternoon, my mother informed me of a job interview that she had arranged for the next day. I never went back to school, and I never saw Steve again. I heard later that they had moved, and his parents had split up.

Chapter 6

I seem to have hit a brick wall, in that nothing from my high school days made any sense. I left school with an attitude not becoming of the adult world. If anything, I was even more confused, and I was hoping that my entry into the workforce, and the freedom that brings, was to give me a new perspective with which to see things. I was taking steps through life that had no direction, no meaning, and no purpose. The only good thing was that I had a job; I was earning money, and time was on my side.

I don't feel much like telling too many more stories. I don't want this to become the autobiography of James Digne. I would like to get back into the psychology of the human behaviour through the eyes of a simple man. That's me, a simple man. As you can imagine, the psychology of this simple man won't be too hard to understand, as opposed to those intellectual freaks with their long-winded explanations for everything, using words that you and I don't understand. I swear that what they write in a paragraph, I could translate into one sentence that you could understand better. They think the whole world's like them.

However, there are a couple of things that I need to share with you, as I feel they are important in the big picture. And as far as your story goes, I don't want you to stop just because I have. I stopped at the age of fifteen, except for these next couple, and I'm sure by the time you matured at eighteen, there were a lot more experiences that influenced your outlook on life and yourself. The whisper used to say that we can be the person of the experience, which means we can allow the event to dictate who we are, or we can use the experience to choose what we want to be or what we want to do about what happened. I guess that means that we could choose to be a victim or not.

I always found that comforting, even though I didn't know exactly what it meant at the time. The way I dealt with things was to bury them in the back of my mind so as not let them affect me too much, which made everything easier to cope with. But still, there was a lot of resentment and bitterness building up.

It was a couple of months into my apprenticeship, and not having had a haircut since that debacle at high school, I came home one day to have my father tell me to get my hair cut. I refused and came home the next day without a haircut, and to my amazement, he said, "Don't come home tomorrow without your hair cut." So I didn't do either. I didn't get my hair cut, and I didn't come home. I knew my mother would be beside herself with worry, but I had a point to prove. I was gone for three days and two nights, with one of those nights spent in a public toilet.

When I finally arrived home, my father said, "Your mother has been worried sick. You still haven't got your hair cut. Make sure you get it cut tomorrow."

I begrudgingly got it cut, but it was the last time I was to have a haircut for seven years.

There's probably no need to describe the incident in more detail, apart from the psychological ramifications. At the time, I was deeply hurt, mainly because of my father's lack of understanding at how important it was for me to look the way I wanted. He was stuck in his old-fashioned ways and was not going to budge, even though the whole world was experiencing fashion fever like never before. For me, it wasn't just about fashion; it was about freedom. It was devastating for a sensitive kid like me; I struggled to deal with it, and I never looked at my father the same way again. I thought that he resented me for the incident, and no matter what I did from that point on, I would never feel as though I was ever good enough for him.

Over the next few months, I was starting to feel the weight of the world on my shoulders. I didn't know why. I had a good job, and I was starting to make more friends and getting interested in girls. I was getting more involved in weekend sports and would still spend time in paradise by the farm. For some reason, I was still shy and becoming more insecure. I continued to lack confidence. This was always a source of frustration, and I felt crippled by it. It wasn't long before I was lashing out and doing crazy things, without knowing why. The reality was that I was screaming out for acceptance and approval, and in some cases, love and understanding. I didn't have any of these things for myself, and my subconscious programme was being put into motion on an unsuspecting world.

There was always a reminder though of where I fitted in within society. I worked with an Austrian man named Felix, who was very moody on occasions. He obviously had some childhood trauma that he hadn't dealt with. One day, not realising how foul he was, I answered him back abruptly when he snarled at me. The next thing I knew, he was grabbing me by my long hair and started to introduce his knee to my nose, several times. A workmate pulled him away before he did too much damage. I don't know what it is with people and my nose. It's not like I stick it anywhere it's not wanted. They all just want to go after it.

That's my last story, for now, and everything else will be just a short mention of what I got up to. I took up surfing with that bunch of mates I was telling you about. I wasn't doing all those crazy things I mentioned earlier on my own, you know. There wasn't any surf inside the bay, so we had to travel north or south, or over to the island. I was spending less and less time in my piece of paradise, but I was discovering another world: nature on a grand scale. The sun, the fun, the surf, the sand, the clothes, the hair, the devil-may-care.

Whilst the experience was fun for me, even though my demons were always close by, there were teenagers drinking, and teenagers crying, and teenagers dying. One of the best lessons for me was watching the personalities of some of these kids change when they were drunk. Many of the guys would get violent and just want to pick a fight, even with their mates. Many of the girls would get emotional and cry about things they didn't want to talk about. Most kids were like me and just wanted to have a good time and be happy. The reality is that we all wanted to do that, but some didn't know how to when they were drunk. Sometimes, we tried to soothe the emotional girls, but that was only because we wanted to get into their pants.

All through life, my youth, my teenage years, and beyond, I always felt that there was something missing, something not quite right, or something more that I was supposed to see or do or be. This was more prevalent during puberty and adolescence, when I was in the rebellion stage. I felt I had been forced to be something I didn't want to be, yet there was no one forcing me to do anything (albeit the rules of society seemed to place restrictions on my freedom). I didn't want to be like my parents or any other grownup I knew. I was different from my brothers, who always seemed to go with the flow.

This created a lot of turmoil within and caused most of the friction between my father and me. I had long hair, wore fancy clothes, and needed space, lots of space. I realise now that it was a sense of self, a sense of knowing who I was, and being the real me that was missing. I was not alone, and my dilemma was like a virus spreading throughout our generation; still, there were some sailing through life with ease (or was it denial?).

If you can have a true sense of self in your life, then all your battles would be over. The battles I'm referring to are the battles with your own demons, the demons created by the many traumatic experiences the subconscious mind has turned into an arsenal of weapons to destroy the truth of who you truly are.

Its arsenal consists of unworthiness, resentment, regret, shame, guilt, and hatred, to name a few. When these deep-seated emotions come to the surface, they can create havoc within society and with other people. These weapons of mass destruction belong to us and are the very feelings we have toward ourselves (albeit on a subconscious level and not known to us on the surface). Even when we become aware of it, the mind transforms that knowing into denial. You, my friends, are in denial, and if that's the way I see you, then that's the way I see myself.

No wonder those young people were either violent or emotional and didn't know why. I had lived a very protective and almost isolated life and actually thought everyone was like me, or at least expected them to be like me: a normal well-adjusted human being. I wasn't sure if I was in control, wanting to be out of control, or out of control and wanting to be in control. It must be always like that when you don't know yourself and are very insecure. I guess the lack of control was a way of releasing any pent-up anger and frustration. Being in control was either denial or very clever camouflage. Either way, neither was healthy in the long term, until it was dealt with on a deeper level.

The stories that I've shared with you so far are merely ripples upon the surface of one's soul, like the gentle breeze across the surface of a lake creating a ripple. It's what lies beneath, in the various depths of the vast exterior of the lake, that matters. I feel like a swim.

I have no doubt that the life we experience from birth into our late teens creates the foundation that supports the structure of the rest of our lives, whether we like it or not, or are aware of it or not. Unless we can go deeper into our own mind and then be able to go beyond the programming that we've been subjected to, it is quite clear that the awareness of our self will never be realised. It can be described as self-knowledge, and not only will it free us of our demons, which we all have on different levels (and if you think you don't, then you're in denial), but it will also benefit the world in general. It may seem like I'm talking in riddles or going around in circles, but I want to stay on the merry-go-round till the penny drops. It's a simple world, and it's worth saving, so we're going to simply save it.

I haven't left our past behind, either; I will be referring back to it on occasions, and not necessarily in a complimentary way. That's not to say that we'll be blaming anyone for our false programming. I call it false only for the reason that we are not living our true selves or our true nature, which in turn places strain on our whole existence. I will explain more on that later.

Getting back to our false programming and our being moulded into society so that we fit into the system, there is no one to blame. We are stuck on a cultural wheel; those before us were subjected to the same beliefs as we were and still are. They are doing the best they can with the limited knowledge they have. I deliberately said limited knowledge because as we gain more and more self-knowledge, we are not restricted to the limited thinking of the past. This is not a criticism of anyone who has influenced our thinking: our parents, schoolteachers, brothers, sisters, uncles, aunts, fellow students, coaches, priests, employers, and of course, all the media outlets: television, radio, newspapers, and magazines. However, it is time to become aware of these influences and make a conscious effort to see through their false messages. I will explain more on that later (it's starting to look like I have a lot of explaining to do).

Becoming conscious of the everyday false images and stories is not that easy when we don't truly know who we are or what we're looking for. Our programming through childhood and the subsequent beliefs we form about the world and ourselves will not allow us to fully understand who we are, or even allow us to be who we are, but to become conscious of who we are not is a major step in transforming us into that which we are. It's vital for our survival on this planet. Denial is destructive, and guilt drives us to destruction. But don't despair; there are no problems, only solutions.

We need to love that part of us that we don't like or cannot deal with; that negative mindset that keeps putting us down and creating thoughts of unworthiness and self-doubt. Know they are there, override them with a conscious awareness, and see them for what they are: a past programme that does not serve any purpose at any stage of one's life. Love your dark side but know that it is not the real you.

Chapter 7

Due to the extraordinary epiphany I experienced when I was forty-nine years old, I found myself in a wonderful position to see the truth of who we are. It is so simple that I could describe it in one word and finish the book right here. However, as with all the simple things in this world, we humans have made them complex, distorted, and unrecognisable. So I have to continue until you people are absolutely sure of your selves.

One magic evening, the whisper showed himself in all his glory, and I found myself engulfed in a mysterious sense of knowing and a great deal of wisdom. From that moment on, I was able to see everything for what it was and found that everything I wanted, needed, or yearned for, I already had. It has been there from the moment I was born and has never left me. It is inside me always, this magic of who we are: peace, bliss, happiness, joy, love, and freedom. That's a pretty big statement, or is it? Haven't we heard it before, many times? Why do we go off into the world trying to find the things that we already have, the most important things we'll ever need?

Well, it's quite simple, really, and this is where the simplicity of our being becomes the focus of a demolition squad. From the moment we're born, they set out to condition us to be like them, and then they programme us to fit neatly into their box of beliefs so that our journey can be smooth and easy, for them. It would be smooth and easy, except they close the lid so that we can't see what goes on outside the box. Once, or if, we finally get to have a look, it becomes very confusing, until we have a change of life experience and, hopefully, an awakening. That is, an awareness of who we are.

I'm angry, people. I know an astute wise man like me should have dealt with his anger by now, and I have, but for your benefit, I am going back there so it's easier for me to explain and for you to understand (assuming, of course, that you haven't dealt with your stuff yet). I'm angry because of all the so-called intellects that over the past centuries have not come up with an education system that promotes self-knowledge from the earliest of ages (that is, from birth). They have been too self-obsessed with making this a better world to live in, for them, while at the same time, they are destroying it, rather than making us better human beings, living in an already beautiful world. We are a very primitive race, people.

I had a vision once of who we truly are; it was quite amusing and also, as I now realise, very insightful. I envisioned letting go of everything: every thought, feeling, emotion, and physical experience that I'd ever had. I removed any tight-fitting clothes so that I could feel comfortable. I took a couple of deep breaths, relaxed every muscle, and let go of all tension in my body. I felt a smile come to my face and then lay down on the floor and started to move my hands around in circles while gently kicking my feet.

It all came so naturally and without any effort. I felt so innocent and blissful that I started giggling, laughing, and talking gibberish: "ga ga gu ga ge ge ga gu da da ge gu" (you get the idea). I thought to myself, *Wow, that is who I truly am.*

I'm just a baby, really, who's been given an instinctive set of instructions for the long road to adulthood. We start off as pure joy, with not a worry in the world: no stress, no anxiety, not one negative thought or feeling (unless, of course, we don't get fed). I felt like I had been reborn and given another chance at life. This experience of an altered state made me wonder if I could get that close to who I was at any given time of my childhood and feel what I was feeling at that time and find out why.

Well, I tried it, and I was able to go into my childhood mind and was horrified. I've never attempted to do that until just now. I only tried it because of the baby realisation. I'm almost stuck for words as I try to find a way of describing the experience. It just explains so much. No wonder I was so timid, was sick a lot, suffered from migraines, had nightmares, and wet the bed for so long. I was such a frightened little child, anxious and stressful all the time. I couldn't actually pinpoint any precise reasons why I would have been like that; so unless it was some karmic debt, I can only assume that it had to be the environment I was being brought up in.

My shyness always held me back, and this caused me to feel inadequate and unworthy at times. I always remember my fear of not being accepted, and I think I spent a lot of time trying to make up for these inadequacies, trying to prove myself worthy. I can understand now, though, why my subconscious was riddled with so much anger and resentment, and also why it made life difficult (or I made life difficult for myself). I thought life was meant to be easy, contrary to what Malcolm once said.

We have got child-rearing all wrong, people. What we are doing to our children is not what our children want or need. I was thrown off-balance by what I discovered. This saving the world thing is not going to be as easy as I thought now. It's still simple; it's just not easy.

Just while we're on parenting, I picked up a wonderful piece of information regarding our parents a few years ago. We actually chose them. I know, I know; it's a hard one to get your head around. I asked myself this question, though: Is anyone going to get hurt or is there any harm in taking on that belief for experimental purposes? I was actually amazed at the results as I thought deep and long about the possibility. If we chose those particular people to be our parents so as to experience exactly what they've offered up, then how do we feel, and what do we think about them now? They certainly did the best they could with the knowledge they had, in which case they played their role perfectly. I discovered a new-found respect for them and will always be grateful for all the lessons I've learnt. It certainly changed my perspective, and I found myself looking at them very differently, even if I didn't believe that I chose them (or did I?). I didn't waste the opportunity to let my children know that they chose me.

Let's go back to that vision of myself as the giggling bundle of joy on the living room carpet and then move into the next few phases of our development, which would be approximately the first three to five years (those years that we don't remember very much); I will attempt to enlighten you, even with the limited vocabulary that I have. I wonder if that can be classed as one sentence. You can tell the intelligence of a person by the length of their sentences, you know.

These are the years, and beyond, when we are discovering ourselves, finding our way, experimenting, learning, experiencing the beauty of the world: the magic of dirt and mud, water and rain, birds and animals, fun, love, joy, and laughter. A parent's role is to feed, shelter, protect, guide, love, and be there. There is no need to educate, train, condition, programme, or brainwash a child into our way of thinking. Every opportunity should be given to children to learn for themselves and not have any beliefs thrust upon them. For example, our us-and-them attitude, winning and losing, good and bad, right and wrong, hero worshipping, our criticisms, judgements, and character assassinations. Being angry at or punishing children in any form must be avoided until they have an absolute understanding of how actions have consequences. All this has the potential to breed guilt, shame, resentment, envy, worry, confusion, anxiety, and fear into a child's mind, which has not developed the skills to cope with emotional pain. Allow children to be themselves and discover their self. We are born with instincts, wisdom, and knowing, and it is the role of parents and society to nurture and enhance these natural attributes of a child.

In fact, our whole education system should be torn apart and redesigned to better accommodate the true nature of who we are. The Industrial Revolution is over, and so should our archaic education system be; it was born out of that period. But you know intellectuals; they know what's best for us, and they want us to either be like them or serve them. My quote: "The simple man is king, and the meek shall inherit the earth. Your research, experiments, and discoveries are trivial compared to the knowledge and wisdom of the human spirit. Your path is a fruitless endeavour, and until you combine your intellect with the will of your soul, the fruits of your labours will be lemons."

Intelligence is a treasure and an asset of great value, but while it contains the ignorance of egoism and the arrogance of self-importance, it will lose touch with the fundamental principles of our existence and erode the very nature of human life. It is then that the mighty will fall, and the meek shall inherit what's left. The innocent are discovering, while the ignorant are in denial.

I'm really getting stuck in here, aren't I? Not only am I waking you up to the behaviour of our intellects, but I'm waking them up to themselves (if that's possible). I am deliberately turning on the anger, judgement, sarcasm, and criticism for the purpose of the message. I'm not really the type of person who goes around passing judgements. It's just that I've read so many books on self-help, personal development, spiritual awareness, mind control, and the power within; there are thousands of books out there that talk about the magic of self. These wonderful books are highly recommended, but they don't seem to be getting the message across. Not enough of them take us to the source of our underlying issues, that is, the real reason in fine detail on why we need to read these books in the first place. Some do, of course, but in a very subtle way. If I'm going to literatureally (added to dictionary) attack some sections of society, it's because I want to wake them from their slumber and bring them into the big picture of saving the world. These books are caring and polite, but I want to take my closed fist and tap gently on the middle of your forehead with the heel of my hand. Wake up. The world needs you now.

As we go through childhood and adulthood sitting in our comfortable box, we are slowly being separated from the truth of who we are, until we start wondering why we are not happy. As I have said; if we don't find out who we are not, we'll never know who we truly are, no matter how much reading we do. Finding one's self is the ultimate awakening, but if we haven't weeded out all the unwanted beliefs and programmes in the subconscious, then falling back into the sewage pit of the mind will always be possible (or, should I say, inevitable).

All our nasty negatives are stuck steadfast to the inner walls of our minds, and they are not going to let go easily. They like who we are and sit comfortably in the knowledge that we are not going to do anything about them. They love it when we're stressed, depressed, anxious, or afraid; they thrive on our addictions, afflictions, illnesses, and pain. All these things are self-inflicted, caused by our false and limiting beliefs about who we are. We become what we think, but we are not who we think we are.

I know that if we find the purest form of who we are, and stand resolute in that being, we will change the world for the better. If we go on through life with the psychological issues that we all have (worse if you are in denial of them), then the chances of saving the world become very slim. I now ask you this question: Can you stand resolute in your purest form?

I think you are starting to get the gist of what I'm doing here. I can't leave any stone unturned in my endeavour to make a change in this world. This is the grand plan in the rebuilding of a new set of beliefs about who we are, and it is absolutely vital that we understand each step that we take along the way. I don't want to keep going round in circles because I'm getting dizzy. If the penny hasn't dropped by now, then please go back to page 1. I tell you this: if you want to change the world, then change yourself, and if you are still wondering about why I got the cuts at high school, then you'll just have to keep on reading.

Now is probably a good time to work on dealing with our unwanted programmes; you know, those series of beliefs that others instilled in us long before we even realised it, child abuse at its ignorant best, not to mention the terrible way we were treated while our young minds were still developing. I know that sounds a little harsh (okay, very harsh), but let's not deny anything; otherwise, we won't get anywhere. And as I've said, this is not about blaming or judging; this is about the facts of what happened at a vulnerable and crucial time of our development. Even if you had the perfect toddler upbringing; this process is not going to harm you; in fact, it will help to give you an insight into everybody else's issues and, hence, the world's issues.

The first seven years of our lives is the time when we form what I will call our blueprint. This blueprint is like a pattern or a template which is rigid in its form. It is a vast web of beliefs that we programme into our subconscious through our everyday experiences. What we see, hear, and feel emotionally is stored deep within our extraordinary little minds. It is the beginning of how we view the world, others, and ourselves. If our subconscious latches onto fear during this period, then we are more likely to see everything very differently, as opposed to it latching onto love. I have no doubt that our blueprint creates the pattern for the rest of our lives, even though we are constantly being conditioned by our parents, schoolteachers, and life itself, beyond our blueprint's formation. What's important here is how we react to or perceive this conditioning, according to our blueprint. The blueprint can't be changed during this conditioning; however, it can be added to.

Let's not forget that our blueprint can be formed with either love and a little bit of confusion, or fear with very little love. I would like to say at this point that even though the blueprint is set in concrete, it can still be counteracted (or at least made insignificant) by a reprogramming of love. If the blueprint was love based in the first place, then the process may not be necessary on a large scale. Let's not forget, though, that love at any time in any measure will never go astray.

Here we are, travelling through childhood, with our blueprint rolled up in our subconscious, with no idea of the true meaning of who we are or what we're doing here. We're being guided by individuals with their own blueprint who are trying to help us get through; our instincts are not nurtured, and our wisdom and knowledge of truth are clouded over with false and limiting beliefs. I can remember my mother saying to me on more than one occasion, "James, I don't know what's going to become of you."

The positive blueprint, that is, the one that has love, bliss, peace, freedom, hugs, kisses, lots of attention, and emotional support as its programme, where children show confidence, wisdom, creativity, compassion, caring, and a sense of connectedness with nature and the environment, need not be emphasised here, as those fortunate beings may not find it necessary to read this book. As my sentences grow, so does my intellect (or is that the other way around?).

However, having just written those inspiring words about positive blueprints, it may be wiser to keep up with that line of thought. When you think about it, we'll definitely find it easier to save the world through our positive outlook and our wonderful sense of self.

I've changed my mind about the fortunate beings (or I prefer love beings) I just spoke of. Maybe it is a good idea if they read this book. After all, they are already saving the world, whether it is consciously or unconsciously. That is their true nature, and they don't know any different; they are probably wondering why so many people are struggling with the simple truths of their existence. This book will explain to them about the different blueprints that exist amongst us and how they, as wiser people, can help others to see beyond the doom and gloom of their inner world. We all know that our outer world is a reflection of our inner world. Don't we?

The negative blueprint is a nasty one, and if children are not reprogrammed with unconditional love and showed compassion and understanding, then the chances of a happy outcome are slim. I'm not saying that no one with a negative blueprint can succeed in life. But I am saying that they will find it difficult, some impossible, to ever find true meaning in their life. I welcome all objections regarding that last statement to be true. You get that?

As adults, it takes a lot of hard work and discipline to change the negative beliefs we have about ourselves, which were formed at such an early age (albeit in our subconscious mind, which I keep stressing). Although I'm not usually into comparisons, I'd like to know how you are travelling compared to the love beings.

Let's focus more on the negative blueprint now, as I feel that this is where most of us have originated from. I speak of false, negative, and limiting beliefs that we acquire through this early programming; they are detrimental to our growth as humans. Instead of becoming love beings, we are more prone to become fear beings.

Some harmless beliefs (although some may not agree with that description) include the Easter bunny, the tooth fairy, Santa Claus, and even the boogie man. There are many more, and some are explained away as fairy-tale figures or imaginary friends. These so-called imaginary friends are a type of escape for children, as it is often too difficult for them to face the reality of their environment (my imaginary friend was real, though).

The not-so-nice beliefs that children form about themselves are created by parents withholding affection or not giving them enough time and attention. Criticising, condemning, and ignoring will always turn children against themselves, as they will believe they are at fault and are not good enough. Children who feel unloved will believe they are unlovable. If we are not shown love, then we will believe that we are not worthy of love. Children will pick up on the moods and even the thoughts of their parents. Children sense interactions between their parents, and if the parents are arguing, they will almost always believe that they are the cause of the fight. Even if children are too young to remember any of the above, the negative emotions will sit in the subconscious, and they will always be affected by it. This also creates abandonment issues (I'll write more on that later).

It is vital for new parents, well before conception, to educate themselves on child-rearing and not rely on their own beliefs or their parents (or grandparents). In fact, it would be wise for all parents and grandparents to learn more about the nurturing of the world's most valuable asset. It is time to change the beliefs around this subject and also change the whole culture regarding the nurturing of newborns through to adolescence. I am not an expert on this subject, but as I've said, there are many who are, as well as many books available. Swami Google will be able to steer you in the right direction. However, I have given you some valuable insight into a child's subconscious mind, and it is your responsibility to create a love being, which is not only what your child deserves but what the world needs.

Our negative blueprint is a subconscious set of beliefs that eat away at our self-belief and destroy our vision of who we truly are. We start seeing ourselves as useless, unloved, unwanted, inferior, unworthy, and resentful; our view of the world becomes an ugly place from this vantage point. But of course, these untrue, unwanted, and undeserved subconscious visions of ourselves are not there to stop us from living, but they do stop us from loving ourselves. It then becomes very difficult to love others if we don't love ourselves.

Chapter 8

Why do I dig up all these childhood issues? Why is it necessary to take this journey into one's subconscious mind? Well, if you remember, it's because some clown said earlier that if we write about our life experiences, it will help us to find out who we are. I feel like I'm getting buried in the manure from the backside of life. I guess if I look on the bright side of that statement, it could mean that if I sow the right seed, it'll grow to be big, strong, and healthy.

Having received some wonderful insight into who I am not, via the whisper, I found myself delving deep into my subconscious mind. I needed to know why we are not living the truth of who we are, when as I now know, it is so close and so simple. Even though my programme still rises up to haunt me on occasions, I am now better equipped to deal with it. I no longer allow it to run my life, the way it used to.

The fear of abandonment as a child is a major cause of mental illness in adulthood. Negative blueprints will always cause problems for adults. The severity of the problems can vary from minor personal traits to serious psychological issues. It is also one of the greatest causes of social dysfunction. Addictions and co-dependency are some of the natural outcomes of repressed emotional pain and childhood abandonment issues.

Behind every person with an addiction, be it drugs, alcohol, gambling, crime, sex, or work, there is a blueprint of low self-esteem, unworthiness, guilt, resentment, and shame. For some, crime is then justified, if they so choose, as they are only finding a means to an end. Desperate people do desperate things, and theft, prostitution, abuse, physical violence, and even murder can become a way of life. It is so easy to judge and criticise these people, and if we're harmed in any way by them, then we are seen to be the victim. They do have mental issues; many psychological conditions are the result of their negative programming. However, their behaviour is not acceptable, and a timeout, whether that be rehabilitation, psychiatric commitment, or a term of imprisonment, is vital for the safety of the community and even themselves.

The point I'm making here is that these people are victims long before they inflict any damage on society. I challenge you to investigate the blueprint of Charles Manson ("Look down at me you see a fool; look up at me you see a God; look straight at me you see yourself"), one of the most infamous mass murderers of the sixties, and you'll find that we are fortunate that a lot more people weren't killed (or that's what they would have us believe). I'm not convinced that he killed anyone, but he certainly was a product of his blueprint, and I'm convinced that with a more positive upbringing, we would be asking, Charles who? Society is programming us long before we have any say in who we want to be or what we want to do. If we don't or can't cope with the way it has to be, then what we want to be will be lost in the maze and turmoil of self-pity and self-hatred.

We start our journey in earnest by attending school, with many going on to university. The expectations upon our school children are enormous. Some cope better than others;

however, all experience anxiety, and it doesn't stop in the academic arena of the classroom.

They have competitive sports to contend with, as well as their artistic expression to enhance. It is wonderful for all kids to experience school and to gain as much knowledge as they possibly can. There are many opportunities that arise from a good education; it can be rewarding, satisfying, and profitable. However, I question a system that neglects children of a lesser blueprint, only to send them into a world they are not ready for and expect them to be upstanding citizens.

One of the factors that cause friction and rebellion in families and society is the way parents raise and prepare children for the world they we were brought up in. The world is changing more quickly than ever before, and it is vital for parents to see the world as it is, which is how our children see it, and not as it was in the past. It doesn't matter how the world is or was; it is more important now than ever for children (and adults, for that matter) to have a better sense of self.

There is enormous pressure on our youth and always has been, whether it is conscious or unconscious, to complete their education, get a job, buy a car, find a spouse, settle down, buy a house, and start a family; it is all part of society's programme to keep the wheels of progress and evolution turning, a programme that worked for a short time but is now failing miserably.

I heard of an incident recently where a man who had just been evicted from his home walked into the real estate office and shot dead the receptionist and himself. He had told a friend earlier that if a man hasn't got a home, then he's got nothing. What sort of society programmes a belief like that into someone? Unfortunately, ours does, and it's time to take responsibility for the system that is programming society and look for alternatives.

When one knows the truth, one sees the illusion, and it's not the prettiest of realisations. When the illusion is exposed, the delusion becomes obvious. Seeing beyond the illusion is the first step to saving the world. In fact, it will become a healing process, the process of healing the world.

More and more people are finding it difficult to deal with their own expectations (and society's). The pressures upon them to live what is perceived a normal life is almost impossible with the internal programme they have running. The outcome that festers from such a negative outlook becomes repulsive to the very society that created it. Like it or not, we are all responsible in some way for everyone's situation in life, whether we know it or not.

The world we live in has been created by our own minds. Everything that happens in life and in the world is created by thought. The cycle of limited thinking by generation after generation is accentuating the problems of the world through fear, ignorance, and denial. One only has to read a newspaper or watch the news on television to see that we are not only killing others but killing ourselves. Our mental state is degenerating at a rapid rate because of our negative blueprints, which perceive a false reality, and our unhealthy diet.

The false media propaganda does not help with one's psychological or spiritual development, either; in fact, the media does more harm than good in its attempt to sensationalise situations with false and misleading reports in its quest to sell advertising. They manipulate trivial events to look catastrophic, just to put more fear into our already overloaded programme. It is so easy for us to sit in the comfort of our lounge and pass judgement or comment on such a crazy, mad world. I can assure you that you are part of this world and therefore part of the problem. If you cannot see that, then you are either ignorant or in denial, or both. I would also like to inform you that you are part of the solution. No. You *are* the solution.

Now, people, I don't want you to sit there reading this, thinking things like, *What an interesting concept; that's a good point he makes. That's a different point of view; hope it goes well for him.* If that's your attitude, then I will be gentle and kind to you by saying, "Go back to page 1, and don't speed-read."

I am not normally a spreader of doom and gloom, but the truth is, doom and gloom exist, and everyone's sitting around, waiting for someone else to do something about it. The fact is that there is something that can be done, but first, everyone has to realise that they are all a part of the problem and therefore have to be part of the solution. Many of us have negative blueprints, through no fault of our own, yet we are not the slightest bit aware of it. Society churns out negative blueprints faster than a mint can print money.

Our system allows most of us to get off scot-free, while others struggle to function within the very society that we have created. The survival of the fittest does not wash when it comes to the survival of human beings. We are all someone's child. I'm not saying that we should invite drug addicts and burglars into our homes for shelter. But it shouldn't be so easy for us to say that it isn't our fault or any of our business.

It is so easy to sit on the throne of denial, to judge, criticise, and point the finger at those who are lost, lazy, or less well off. We ourselves are in the midst of our many belief systems, working within a maze of programmes within our subconscious.

I can't stress enough how important it is for us, as so-called intelligent people, to break this cycle of self-imposed psychological, emotional, physical, and spiritual destruction. It has to be our prime focus from now on to reprogramme society, starting with the education of our young through to the mature. Forget about scientific research, experiments, and technological advancement; it will all come to no avail if the planet becomes a mental institution.

The saving of the world cannot be achieved by one, but it can be done if we are all one, united in our efforts to conquer hatred and fear. As I've said before, it's not easy, but it is simple.

When you intend to save the world, it makes it difficult when you are a fear being whose foundation is a negative blueprint.

Chapter 9

I have already touched on our education system, which is all about programming minds rather than educating people. As parents, we all want the best for our children, and that means a good education as well. However, if our own education left out such vital lessons around self-knowledge and self-awareness and failed to enhance our self-expression and self-confidence, then we won't expect our children's education to be any different, because we don't know any better, and so the cycle continues.

Our programming and lack of education is creating psychological issues in some areas; a lot of our physical problems are the result of mental trauma. The negative blueprint which results in low self-esteem, anger, hatred, fear, resentment, and bitterness causes anxiety and stress, which eventually causes physical sickness and disease (or dis-ease). In fact, I'd be confident in saying that stress, in one form or another, is the cause of most of our physical illnesses. The greatest killer of any living creature is stress. The human body is such that the mind and the physical are so closely connected that they react to each other's stress and illnesses.

This mind-body connection is so powerful, yet it is the pharmaceutical companies, with their enormous profits and influential political clout, who would not have the human race healed with anything but the chemical compounds that they research, patent, and mass-produce. This is where our intellectuals are duped into believing they are doing wonders for other people.

There are people throughout the world, including children, dying from drug trials performed by pharmaceutical companies. Scientific researchers have studied long and hard to obtain a well-paid job in a field where they think they are serving humanity. Many universities are subsidised by pharmaceutical companies. It's becoming obvious day by day that more and more people are being prescribed more and more drugs and medicines, not to mention the eagerness to get them to the operating table. I'll leave the research and the ramifications of all that for you to explore.

It seems to me that the unhealthier we are, through the many illnesses and diseases, the more chance we are of being exploited. We become vulnerable and are at the mercy of the medical profession and the powerful drug companies.

I'm not that naïve that I don't realise it's all about the bottom line, the shareholders, being in the black. In fact, it's all about money and profit. In the eyes of the multinationals and their subsidiaries, the welfare of the human race has become less important than the acquisition of money.

It must be said right now that my comments are not meant to judge anyone. It's just the way it is, and we are all following a system, a pattern, a template that to me is not conducive to saving the world. I'm making everyone aware that the system is not ideal for our long-term survival. The area I know will be of most benefit for a healthier human race is diet and stress management. The food we eat and the stress we are under are killing us. As adults, we have no excuse once we become aware of these simple facts. Unfortunately, the problem stems from a blueprint that has us believe we are getting what we deserve and this is our lot in life. If I thought that was only affecting the people who believed it, or if it was a minority group, then I would say good luck to them. The truth is, that way of thinking affects the whole of humanity in a negative way. I will discuss more on that later.

The further I delve into this mystery, the closer I feel I'm getting to solving the problems of the world. Don't you think so too? Well, I'm getting to understand my blueprint a bit better, and I feel I am closer to revealing who I am not.

Religion would have us believe that solving the problems of the world could be done through God, and that may be so for some, but it has been tried for thousands of years without success. Maybe if they worked with the truth rather than fear, sin, and greed, they would be more successful. The squabble over who is or was the true Son of God is so trivial compared to the truth about God, which seems to be overlooked by those who don't really want us to know. I won't go down that track, but if you want, there are many books on the subject, as I keep saying. Besides, this is all about combatting the subconscious mind. My battle with God will have to wait; I don't want my keyboard to blow up.

The government's answer would be for us all to be honest, work hard, and vote for them: to pay our wage tax, company tax, payroll tax, fuel tax, our land rates, stamp duty, water bill, power bill, health insurance, superannuation, vehicle registration and insurance, school fees, union fees, and interest rates. There is also a tax on alcohol, tobacco, and many other consumer items. I can never understand why countries that have so many natural resources are always in debt and have to rely heavily on taxing their own population.

We have got it wrong, people, when one company (and sometimes a foreign company at that) can reap our natural resources for profit, while we sit back and pay taxes to keep the government afloat. Is that mismanagement, or could there be something more sinister happening here on a grand scale? I can see fear, greed, and sin hovering like vultures around this concept that we call free enterprise.

If the truth be known, there is enough money, natural resources, land, food, and water to satisfy the population of the whole world. There is no need for any human being to go without; in fact, our whole existence here is to enjoy this fabulous planet and to serve it the best we can. We are not servants, but we are here to serve. It's time to ask why we are being suppressed, brainwashed, misled, and herded like sheep into barren pastures that are not beneficial to us.

There seems to be a sinister plot brewing throughout the world that is designed to keep us captive in our own minds. The system has been set up for the rich to prosper, rule, and manipulate, and the unsuspecting armed forces keep it that way.

The world's banking cartel can be seen as the cause of humanity's woes, which includes our quality of life. Our whole existence within the framework of society is based on our financial position. Freedom from the financial strain and the heavy cost of living has to be close to everyone's goal, and that is understandable, considering the programme we are attuned to. As I said earlier, there is enough to go around, including money, and it's not as if we haven't earned it.

There is speculation throughout the world of a forthcoming governing body called the New World Order. Associated with this body are the members of the Freemasons Lodge, which have been closely related to the Illuminati. If there is uprising in the streets by the citizens of democratic countries, and martial law is the result, then I would suspect that their agenda is more of a national socialist regime.

If the Illuminati are controlling the financial institutions of the world, as is the speculation, then their influence on the world economy is most important to us all. The question is, do they want us all to prosper, or do they want to control the world and therefore control us? They are very wealthy, powerful, and influential people, and not only do they control the flow of money throughout the world, but their interests and influence include the education system, religion, government, oil, defence, media, and pharmaceuticals, just to mention a few. People working in these fields would be totally oblivious to the agenda of the Illuminati and are usually labelled by the hierarchy as "useful idiots."

The Illuminati is based in the centre of London. Much has been written about them, and it has been suggested that they orchestrated the two world wars (and a third is on the way). They also want to create a world government to ensure that no nation prints their own money or defaults on a loan, and therefore protect their monopoly over government credit, our credit. I see the three uglies rising again: fear, greed, and sin (and we're worried about natural disasters).

If the world is to have a governing body, then I hope for everyone's sake they are there for a good cause and to bring peace to the planet. We cannot wait to find out, so I'll press on with my battle with the subconscious.

While writing this section, I received a posting on my Facebook site of rap singer Eminem, who'd written a song about the Illuminati and the New World Order, with the title of "Wake Up." If it gets played by mainstream media outlets, it will be a good thing. It will be interesting to see if the powers that be will allow its promotion. There are many books written on the Illuminati and the New World Order, and none of them portray the Illuminati as a group that promotes the welfare of humanity or is willing to bring peace to the world.

Their reptilian blueprint of nothing or no one matters if it doesn't benefit them is programmed deep into their sinister minds. I was mistaken for thinking that they'd save the world. We are playing right into their hands by creating a dysfunctional society through ignorance and our own greed, fear, and sin. When it becomes impossible for us to control our behaviour through our inability and not knowing who we are, then it opens the doorway for reptilian predators to wipe us off the face of the earth any way they can. It looks like I have another battle on my hands. Maybe if I pray, then God will take care of them.

I've just given some of my informed views regarding a few subjects, and no doubt there will be a few who will refute these comments. All I can say to them is pick up a newspaper or watch the news or a current affairs show with your eyes and your mind open. If you can look beyond the sensationalism, they are still stories about a human race that is not functioning as it could. The world would change in an instant if all the stories were positive, happy, and uplifting. In time, it would even help to sell more advertising.

We are creating this world, which we regard as our reality, by our unconscious and subconscious minds. What you think, you create. The more negative the thinking, the more negative the creation. The negative thinking runs parallel to our negative blueprints, which in turn makes everything seem normal. It's only when we wake up to the truth and see the illusion of this reality, then we can change our thoughts and beliefs to create a more positive outlook. But it must begin with looking inward before we can change our outward view of the world and therefore transform it.

Chapter 10

There is a great opportunity in the early years of schooling to rewrite the blueprint, but it seems that we are too occupied with educating the child to suit our archaic way of thinking and living. The education system is neither relevant nor appropriate to their psychological, emotional, and creative needs. The expectations and stress placed upon our children throughout our structured school system does not allow them to grow with a healthy sense of self. The spiritual aspects of one's being, which is among the most vital parts of a child's nurturing, is ignored at the most vital stage of development. Measuring their academic skills and competing between others becomes more important than the truth of who they are.

Our own programming does not allow us to see the big picture clearly enough to allow us to make the changes to a child's early learning experiences that are necessary so that our society can provide a more psychologically and emotionally stable environment.

Some five-year-olds have negative blueprints they need attending to before we should even attempt to thrust our inadequate education programme upon them. Their sense of self has been clouded over or masked by a false identity that we have imposed upon them. Their true nature has been buried so deep that it is almost non-existent, and we expect these children to then learn things they don't need to know.

As I've said, we are born with everything we need to know. As soon as we are taken away from the concept of self, we start to forget the truth of who we truly are. The new knowledge that we gain through the teachings of the tribe overshadows and at times destroys that knowledge, which is our birthright. It is an unknown knowledge which is only known when we know our self.

What we need to understand as human beings is that if the truth of who we are is nurtured, allowed to grow, and encouraged to develop within us, then teaching external knowledge would be easier and a lot more fun to learn. Our unlimited potential, that is, the enormity of who we are, would not be denied by our false and limited conditioning, which is thrust upon us by others with false and limiting beliefs. There is an undiscovered frontier within us that is beyond comprehension, beyond our wildest dreams or our most glorious imaginings. Our ignorance and fear have entrapped a timeless and endless wilderness of wonder within us, which is bursting to reveal itself.

We are here to nurture that which our children already know through their instincts and intuition, and to teach them what they want to know, without secret agendas or high expectations (without any expectations). Any word, deed, or thought from another which creates anxiety can have long-lasting effects in how children see themselves and the world. Children will always see themselves as perfect, unless we teach them otherwise.

My experience in front of the class in grade one to debate the pin and needle seems so insignificant now, but at the time, it was a major setback in my development in becoming a socially interactive child. It just added to the already existing negative view I had of myself and helped to keep my blueprint intact. In fact, I unconsciously created the experience so as to justify my lack of self-worth. There'll be more on that later.

I feel like a soapbox is being eased under my stance, the pose that holds resolute wherever it goes. I might have some fun for a while, people; come with me. I too have stepped into my greatness and realised my genius, and I stand at the apex of humanity, watching the world of the many suffer at the hands of the few. I may be at the height of a thousand soapboxes, but I am not above anyone. I want you to rise with me and stand resolute in who you are, not in who you are not.

The simplicity of who we are has been overshadowed by the chaos and madness created by our own minds through the construction of the great delusion. They want us to be in debt. They want us to be sick. They want us to be dysfunctional. They want us to be at war. They want us to do drugs, steal from each other, and kill each other and ourselves. They want us to smoke too much, drink too much, screw too much, and crash planes, trains, and automobiles. Do you really think they care? They're not going to allow us to be who we are. If they do that, then they will lose control over us.

I say we say, enough is enough. We have to allow ourselves to be who we are. You have to be aware of the delusion before you can realise the illusion.

Chapter 11

"Jean!" I hollered at the top of my voice, thinking there was no one around for miles.

A voice came from the bush: "She's dead, mate."

I was horrified as Tim Fenton appeared from nowhere. "Who's dead?" I asked.

"Jean Brown," he answered.

"How do you know Jean Brown?" I asked.

"She was in my class at high school, you dickhead," he replied.

"Oh, yeah," I said.

Jean had been gone for about eighteen months, and I felt it was time to open up a little; besides, I had been caught off guard, and I didn't want him to think I was crazy.

"I fantasise about her a lot, you know," I said. "I pretend she's still alive, living in a tent in the bush here. I visit her in my dreams at night. She has a campfire going and sits by it while waiting for me to arrive. She wears a slinky white dress with nothing underneath. She leads me into her tent, takes off her dress, and lies naked on a sheepskin rug, allowing me to caress her all over."

"You're giving me a hard-on, Jimmy," Tim commented. "Man, you have to let her go, or you'll go crazy."

"I'm okay," I said. "In some strange way, I find solace in her peace."

Jean and I never had sex in my dream. I would sit with her and admire her naked beauty whilst touching her tenderly. She would look up and smile occasionally and say how nice it felt. I didn't think there was any harm in it, and anyway, it was only a dream. Calling out her name felt a bit weird, but I wanted to know what it was like to hear her name. I didn't really care if no one understood, but then, no one was supposed to know.

Tim was a year or so older than me and lived on the main road, a couple of miles from the farm. We used to hang about together on the weekends a few years ago. He told me a bit about the human anatomy, both male and female. He explained to me the other use for the penis and how it all worked, so we sort of bonded in a way. He was much more into that sort of stuff than I was. He had two sisters who were much older than him, so I suppose that was how he got most of his information.

We had a falling out back then over the raft I was building. He stormed off after I told him it was my timber, my drums, my raft, my way, so if you don't like it, lump it. It wasn't like me to get that angry at anyone, but I was over spoilt brats and didn't like his engineering-type ways of building things. I liked things simple. He built a billy cart once that used a steering wheel from an old car, as opposed to a piece of string. The problem was that when you turned the wheel to the right, the cart went left, and vice versa.

I couldn't drive the thing, so I asked him why he just didn't tie a piece of string to each side of the axle and use that to steer. He said he wanted it to look like a real car and added that he could drive it okay. So when he tried to tell me how to build a raft, I had to let him know how I felt. My mother was proud of me for standing my ground and fighting for my rights. I thought I was being stubborn, obnoxious, righteous, selfish, and a little childish, but I didn't care.

It was good to catch up with Tim after so long. We had some good discussions, but he always did most of the talking. He seemed to be obsessed with sex, and that was the content of most of our talks.

"I went skinny-dipping in the creek last weekend with my cousins," he told me. "I almost got a hard-on then too."

"You haven't changed a bit," I replied jokingly. "Was it Mark and Tom?"

"No, you dickhead," he snapped. "Mary and Julie."

Mark and Julie were from one family, and Tom and Mary another, and they lived two and three doors up from Tim.

"You mean Mary and Julie took their gear off?" I gasped.

"No, only me; they both piked it, although I'm sure Julie wanted to," he said.

"Oh, you're a pervert," I replied. "Hey Tim, let's do something crazy."

"I don't do crazy, Jimmy, but tell me your plans anyway," he said.

"I don't have any plans, Tim, but how about you ask the girls if they want to skinny-dip again? They might take their clothes off this time. I'll hide behind the bushes."

"No. They won't do it because they don't want to swim in the creek. It's too murky for them."

"Fair enough," I said.

After a long pause, I confessed to Tim that I thought I loved Jean, and I would have married her.

"If you don't stop, Jimmy, you'll go stark raving mad," he said.

"No, I won't," I replied. "It feels safer this way than if it was real."

"You have to get yourself laid, Jimmy," he remarked, "and as soon as possible,"

"That's your answer to everything, Tim. Have you ever been laid? Don't lie to me?"

"No, not really; well, once maybe. My sister and I messed about late one night. She was a bit tipsy, and I was a bit horny, so one thing led to another. It wasn't really sex. We just played around with each other."

I decided not to go down that track with Tim and hoped he would change the subject, and he did.

"Hey, Jimmy, I have another confession," Tim announced.

"Oh, yeah? Do I need to hear this?" I replied, thinking it was going to be another one of his depraved stories.

"Well, it concerns you, but I don't want you to interrupt till I finish," he said.

"Okay. Spill your guts," I replied.

"Do you remember that dickhead prefect at school, Paul Roberts?" he asked.

"Yes," I answered. "And his little sister," I added.

Tim began his story: "Well, he caught me carving his initials [I wanted to interrupt and ask why his initials, but then it made sense] into the back of a seat on the bus. He didn't say anything, but I knew the bastard was going to dob me in when we got to school. Then you started blowing rice at everyone through your pen. [I was listening intently but wasn't sure if I was going to like where this ended up.] When we were getting off the bus, the driver told Roberts to report you to the headmaster. That's when Roberts came up to me and said that if I reported you, then he wouldn't report me."

"So it was you, ya dickhead," I snapped. "Why didn't he just report both of us?"

"I asked him that question as well, and he said that he thought you were crazy enough to seek revenge, like burn his house down or rape his little sister."

"Tell me you're joking, Tim," I said.

"You had him bluffed, Jimmy."

I sat there for a few minutes, horrified that anyone would think that I could do something like that.

"What an idiot," I finally said. "I hate intellects. They're so stupid. His sister's ugly, anyway."

Tim started to laugh and then said, "Have you seen her lately, Jimmy? She's hot."

We both began laughing, and then I leaned over, punched him solidly on the arm, and said, "That's for dobbing me in, dickhead."

"Why would someone like that want to kill herself?" I asked, thinking out loud. "She had so much to live for."

"They reckon she'd been molested or raped, but wouldn't tell anyone about it. Everyone knew that, even her brother Steve."

I let out a huge moan of disbelief and then said, "What? How come I didn't know that? Why am I always the last to be told anything?" Actually, deep down, I think I knew that and had my suspicions around who raped her too.

Tim didn't say anymore, as I think he realised how harsh he'd just been. He was still at high school after I'd left, so I suppose he'd been through all the gossip and innuendo, and was totally over it. I guess I did know what happened; who knows? Maybe I knew more than most but didn't want to face up to it. If she'd just talked about it to someone and relieved the burden, then things may have been totally different. But what if it was her father who was having sex with her, and her mother knew about it but didn't want her to tell anyone? Where did that leave Jean?

I was starting to realise that Tim was right; it was time to let her go. Talking about it, or at least broaching the subject with Tim, made me see that my obsession with Jean was starting to affect my mental state.

I got up to walk home, took a few steps, and then turned to Tim and said, "Jean who?"

He smiled and replied, "See you around, hey."

"Yep, see ya, mate," I said. As I walked off, a feeling of intrigue came over me. I turned and called out, "Hey, Tim. What were you doing down this part of the creek, anyway? You weren't gonna pinch my crab pots, were you?"

"No," he replied. "I needed to go for a long walk. I'm thinking of asking Jan Roberts, Paul's sister, out on a date, and I'm not sure if it's a good idea or not."

"Go for it," I said. "If she says no, we can always burn her house down."

We both laughed and went our separate ways.

I knew the track back to Tim's place, as we'd walked it several times. Even though we lived so close, the bushland was much thicker than mine. The trees and the vegetation were different as well. There were large gum trees, wattle trees, and different types of eucalypts, whereas I'd be walking through mangroves, she-oaks, tea trees, and paperbarks.

As I wandered back home through the droopy she-oaks, I felt the burden of Jean's death lift from my shoulders. The heavy weight that I'd been carrying for so long suddenly disappeared. My welfare was more important than anything else that was happening around me. It was such a significant and monumental transformation that I began to wonder if my running into Tim had been orchestrated, rather than a coincidence. I felt content and put it down to the presence of the whisper. Could this reverent whisper have sent me a messenger in the form of Tim Fenton? Stop it, James.

Chapter 12

It was time to have some fun, fun, fun. I was earning money now, and that seemed to give me some independence which was hard to get used to, but once I did, whoa.

I also re-established friendships with mates I'd gone to primary school with but who'd gone on to different high schools. These were exciting times, and we all seemed to be in the same frame of mind, if you know what I mean. It was the 1970s. What else do I have to say?

It was the beginning of my cutting loose from the conformities of society. I was beginning to understand the hippies a lot better but wasn't prepared to go down that track. With my long hair, flared pants, thongs, and mango T-shirt, I was often referred to as a hippie by those still out of touch with reality. I preferred the term "surfie" better, but it still wasn't appropriate. We much preferred to be called surfers. What better place to meet one's future wife than on the beach, happy, tanned, and sober.

Speaking of alcohol, things haven't changed, with all the binge-drinking we did. It was mostly Friday and Saturday nights, with surfing during the day on Saturday and Sunday. It became a way of life, a culture, a habit, and it wasn't always pretty, as I mentioned earlier.

My first experience with alcohol was when I was sixteen; against my will, a bottle of rum was shoved in my mouth and poured down my throat. There was a caravan park at the end of Pencil Point, and a couple of brothers and their little sister lived there. They were a couple of rough dudes and did a bit of fishing in the bay. One of my mates claimed their little sister as his girlfriend, which meant we had to associate with these characters. Fred wasn't too bad, but Mick was a mongrel of a man. He was short, wiry, and all muscle, with the meanest look I'd ever seen. He had a reputation for being very violent, and I wasn't comfortable with the arrangement. Rumour was that he'd beaten up four of the local coppers whilst in a drunken rage. My experiences with different characters whilst hitchhiking left me with no doubt that he could have beaten up more.

I was down at the jetty one day, not realising they were there, when they spotted me. There was no escape; they started up the small talk, unbeknown to me, with an ulterior motive. Before I knew it, I was helping them to untangle their fishing net, which was no easy task. Suddenly, they walked off and left me to finish the job on my own. They took my pushbike with them and wanted me to have a drink with them in their caravan before I left. I had no choice but to satisfy their request. I had no choice because Fred shoved the bottle in my mouth and poured.

The rum tasted like poison, but I dared not refuse their hospitality. I knew I had to escape at the earliest opportunity, as being there when they were drunk was not a good idea. All my excuses to leave fell on deaf ears, and I was becoming very anxious. Eventually, I had to risk offending them and became very assertive. I waited till the doorway was clear and moved quickly through it while thanking them and explaining that if

I didn't get home soon, I'd be in a lot of trouble. They weren't happy, but I gave them little time to respond, and I was gone.

A few months later, my mate had broken their little sister's heart. I only found out while on my way to another friend's house, when he and two other mates were lying beside the road, moaning and groaning. If I'd been a few minutes earlier, I would have copped the same. They were battered and bruised but okay, and I remember thinking how very lucky they were to come off so lightly. I could only assume that their little sister's heart was not a major concern for the brothers, only their family pride.

We made a pact after that. In fact, we made many, mostly silly stuff about what type of girlfriend we'd have. No girl with older, angry brothers was at the top of the list, with their parents having to like us all. She had to get on with all of us (that's get on, people, not get it on). She had to have a friend or a little sister. There was other stuff, but you don't really need to know.

Even though it was a lesson for us all, we didn't take the pact seriously, and I think we all broke it within a week. I was still a bit of a loner and liked to go my own way with girls. Even though we were all trying to get a bit, I was more inclined to show more respect for them and was just happy with their friendship. I was still a very shy person and had to operate within those limitations.

By the time I was seventeen, I'd had my heart shattered twice. It has to be the most painful … I don't need to explain. You understand.

It changed me in so many ways, and I was never interested in an emotional involvement after that, vowing to never get married. Even though I still respected the opposite sex, I'd lean towards the wombat way, as a friend once put it. You know: eats, roots, and leaves.

But that never lasts long; human nature (or is it human programming?) interferes, and we end up with a mate, a friend, a lover, a wife.

My social skills were built on a foundation of shyness, and my actions and personality were driven by my insecurities. I tried my hardest and did my best, but there was always something not quite right. I was not equipped with enough self-esteem to have a successful relationship. What one puts into a relationship is what one gets back.

I sometimes wondered why I bothered. Why do we go out into the wide world in search of the perfect mate? Surely, they will come to us when we are in the right place at the right time. What if Toni (the grade one girl I harassed on the way to school that morning) was to be my future wife, and I missed an opportunity?

I remember a story I heard once about a field of diamonds. One day, a man who owned a log cabin on a beautiful pristine property with a freshwater creek flowing through it heard of a field of diamonds discovered in the next state. His family convinced him to sell his property and travel to the field of diamonds to make his fortune. He worked hard for years, but then his money ran out; he returned to his family, penniless, only to find out that during a recent flood, the banks of the creek on the property he'd sold was covered with diamonds.

I'm leaning towards Sue Banks, the sexy fourteen-year-old who offered me sex at high school.

Chapter 13

All through my seventeenth year, I was waiting to get my driver's licence. I was over hitchhiking everywhere, or catching a bus or train, or bumming a lift off my mates.

Hitchhiking home from work every afternoon was an absolute pain. It was scary at times and always risky. I became streetwise during those years, as some of my lifts were unsavoury-looking characters with personalities to match. I had to let go of the shy boy image and always be assertive, direct, and at times act a little crazy. I'd pick my mark though, as I didn't want to frighten them, or they'd never pick me up again.

There was this one guy who picked me up often, and the first and only words he would say to me were, "Another day older, closer to death." I never knew how to respond to that, so I always said nothing. It wasn't a quote that resonated with my way of thinking.

I worked about fifteen miles from home, but when one is sixteen years old, that can seem like a hundred. Fortunately, I never walked the whole way, as a lift always came along. I can remember the problem I had with dogs. I got to know where the vicious ones lived, so I always crossed the road when passing their territory. I made sure I had a big stick in my hand as well.

One day, though, I was walking past unknown territory when suddenly, this nasty dog came running through the property gates, barking and growling at me. I didn't have my customary stick, and he was too close to me to make a run for it. The only thing I could think of was to wait till he got close enough and then kick him under the chin. Well, what would you do?

I connected pretty well, but my thong flew off and landed on the driveway. The next quick decision was; get the hell out of there, which I did. I spent the next ten minutes wondering what I was going to do with only a left-footed thong.

With the experiences I had with the Kerrigans' dog and the many I encountered during my hitchhiking days, it's no wonder that I've never been able to get close to dogs, even though I've had a couple as pets. The first one had to be put down because of distemper, and the next one I gave away because it growled at everyone who walked by. It would always amaze me that some people could approach any dog, even though it was barking and growling at them, and start patting it, only to see the animal wag its tail with joy. I'm almost certain there's a fear factor in there somewhere.

I said earlier that we create our own realities with our thoughts. Most of these thoughts are subconscious and stem from our programme or blueprint. The things we say and do are born out of our thoughts, and many times, they are beyond our control. How many times have you said, "I can't believe I said that?" or "I can't believe I did that?" or "What was I thinking?" These are unconscious moments driven by your subconscious mind, which has been programmed by external experiences.

What on earth has this got to do with being attacked, chased, or bitten by a dog, I hear you say? Well, I reply, much more than you may realise. I will cover it in more detail later, as I have only just scratched the surface of this enormous and complex subject. Don't worry; I'll keep it simple, people. There are exciting times ahead; trust me.

I got off track again, but I have to follow where my mind leads me. I can't help thinking, though, looking back at my life, whether most of the decisions I made were because of my subconscious programming (or at least influenced by it). Did I have that much of a low opinion of myself that I wanted to be attacked by a dog?

Okay, so there I am. I finally got my driver's licence, on the second attempt. I gotta tell ya, people, that I don't mention all the times that I got frustrated and angry, but I was capable of being an angry young man at times. After I'd failed my first attempt, this was one of those times. What was this officer thinking? Did he not know the miles I'd walked, the dogs that had attacked me, the dragons I'd slain, the thongs I'd lost, the lonely drivers I'd endured who were waiting for death? The most incredible feeling of freedom came over me the day that licence was handed to me. The next chapter in my life was about to begin, and nothing was going to stop me from doing what I wanted, when I wanted.

All of a sudden, I seemed to have more friends; there were more girls, more places to go, and it was easier to get there. I suddenly realised that this was more than a driver's licence; this was a licence to live and to love, if you know what I mean.

My health improved, and I'd outgrown the pimple stage. Who invented pimples, by the way? They would have to be one of the greatest contributors to people's low self-esteem. The teenage body needed its burgers and milkshakes, though.

A licence is not much good without a car, or in my case a van, a van that had two single beds; not a station wagon, you know, a van. It was great to have somewhere to sleep while away on weekend surfing trips. Before the van, we always found somewhere to sleep, but it wasn't always comfortable: in a tent, in the dirt, under someone's house. A lot of houses in beach areas were on two-foot-high stumps, so it was always a bit of a squeeze. It was much safer if no one was home, of course.

We'd sleep under the stars at times and hope that it wouldn't rain. This was an issue on the island, as there were wild brumbies to contend with. A mate awoke one night screaming that a brumby was standing over him, two legs either side of his torso, while it was fossicking for food. I think the brumby got the bigger fright that night. We had to rethink our sleeping strategies after that. The ultimate sleeping arrangement was when a young girl rented a motel room for the weekend. The beauty of this was that she always came with at least one friend. I managed to do this one evening but had to apologise because I drank too much and wet her bed.

The van was heaven and very popular with my mates. I had one mate we nicknamed Stud. He would always be the first to ask if he could borrow my car keys. It was always halfway through the evening, and he'd always be back before closing time to have a few beers. I don't know how he did it. He wasn't that good looking. Okay, he was cute, with a great smile, and he had what the girls called "come to bed" eyes.

I sometimes wondered what the girls were all about. I never dwelled on it too much, though, because trying to work girls out at that age would have driven me around the bend. There was no set pattern to their behaviour. One couldn't categorise them like one could a male. It seemed to me that the guys were all the same, but the girls were different from one another. I guess the best way to put it would be to say that most of the guys were after the same thing, but the girls were looking for different things.

I got out of that pretty well, don't you think? I don't have to go into a big explanation about it; otherwise, this would end up a novel. I'm just giving you my perspective on the situation during my generation. I don't know what it was like for other generations, but I certainly wasn't complaining.

I want to tell you now about an incident that happened not long after I got my licence; it shed a light on an earlier tragedy but also took me into darkness I wasn't prepared for. One night, I was visiting a girl I knew, Tracey Stevens, and we were talking over her front fence, when her older sister came running down the stairs in a state of hysteria. It reminded me instantly of the episode with Jean Brown.

I was taken back a bit, when suddenly her mother came out and screamed, "I'll kill us all if you tell anyone."

I asked Tracey what was going on, thinking that maybe it was time to leave. She replied very matter-of-fact, "The old man's been screwing her."

I was horrified and didn't know what to do or say. I decided to be cool, even though my thoughts went straight to Jean

Brown at high school, mainly because Tracey's sister reminded me of her.

I said to Tracey, "And you?"

She replied, "He wouldn't dare touch me."

I'm not sure if she would have told me even if he had. On my way home, I couldn't help but parallel the event with Jean's episode at high school, and I wondered. I just wondered.

The incident awakened my demons that were sleeping so soundly. I humoured them for a while and then calmly put them back to bed, until I got to a time in the future when I could better deal with them. Sexual abuse takes a lot of understanding and even more forgiveness, and I wasn't ready to do either. My own experience left me with a lot of resentment, guilt, and anger. I felt hollow and small so much so that I spent most of my adult life trying to prove myself, not to anyone in particular; it was just a roller-coaster ride of never-ending emotional confusion. You can suppress the pain so deep that you don't even know why you are suffering. The instincts born out of a negative blueprint take over, and you want to show the world you are better than you think you are.

Chapter 14

I rarely visited the bush anymore, and life was so hectic that I hardly ever heard the whisper, or I wasn't listening.

One Sunday morning, a couple of mates came over home, so I took them for a walk along the beach on the eastern side of the farm. One of them pulled out a joint and proceeded to light up. It was the first time for me, and I had no idea what to expect.

It was a pleasant experience, and I found myself giggling a lot and telling this guy that he was a bastard. Although it felt good, I'd lost control and was constantly trying to behave, well, normal. It was time for lunch, and when we got back home, my mother surprised me by inviting my friends for lunch. The bastards weren't going to pass up a free meal, and I was still too stoned to give a damn. By this time, I had managed to stop calling him a bastard, but I still had the giggles. My mother never mentioned the incident her entire life, but I just knew she knew.

I rarely did drugs in my life. It's true; I just didn't feel the need. There was this inner voice (mmm, that's interesting) which was telling me to get drunk instead. No, no, it just didn't feel right for me, and there was too much to do rather than sit around all day and get stoned.

It has always amazed me that I never got more heavily involved in drugs because it was always around and always available, and nearly everyone was doing one thing or another. The guys I hung around were much the same as me, so I suppose this was a positive influence. We just wanted to surf, get a tan, meet the chicks, and sometimes get drunk.

Don't get me wrong; there was a seedy side to surfing in the seventies, but we didn't want to know. Drink driving wasn't as publicised as it is now, but there were kids, guys and girls, getting killed in car and motorbike accidents. There were drug addictions and alcoholism, violence, rape, theft, and even murder.

One of the girls who broke my heart had a brother who became a good friend of mine. I hadn't seen much of him since the breakup, but when I heard on the radio that he'd been murdered and his body burnt; it was a shock, a very difficult time. He was a very cheeky young man, as I remember. He would walk up to a girl on the beach with a matchbox in his hand. In the box was a little wood screw, so on opening it, he would ask if they wanted a screw. Only he could get away with that.

I wanted to contact her but just couldn't bring myself to. I knew how inseparable they were; I felt for her for a long time. Still do.

The seventies. Oh, the seventies. It's great to remember the past, but one shouldn't dwell there forever. It was kind of like a leftover legacy from the sixties. We didn't learn from the mistakes, but we did improve on them. The seventies were not just about taking drugs; it was overdosing on them. The music industry took off so quickly, and soon there were high-quality singers and bands right across the world. I'm focusing on music here because it was the most influential part of my life as a teenager. It was obviously a lifestyle that a lot could not deal with.

We lost Janis Joplin, Jimmy Hendrix, Keith Moon, Tim Buckley, and Elvis Presley. There was Danny Whitten (Crazy Horse), Gary Thain (Uriah Heep), Gram Parsons (Byrds), John Bonham (Led Zeppelin), Sid Vicious (Sex Pistols), Tommy Bolin (Deep Purple), Billy Murcia (New York Dolls), and Vinnie Taylor (Sha Na Na). I don't know about you, but I think this is too many; it ended up being just an entrée for the generations to come.

It was the decade of Neil Young, CCR, the Beatles, Simon and Garfunkel, Pink Floyd, Deep Purple, Aerosmith, ABBA, AC/DC, Billy Joel, Elton John, Rod Stewart, Marvin Gaye, Fleetwood Mac, the Bee Gees, Queen, Led Zeppelin, Clapton, Dylan, James Taylor, Joe Cocker, Carly Simon, the Doors, Don Mclean, Carole King, Stevie Wonder, the Rolling Stones, the Who, Michael Jackson, T Rex, Springsteen, Kiss, and Chicago. Should I mention Osho and the Orange People? The list could go on and on and on. I didn't mean to have such a long list, but I just couldn't stop.

I'd love to write more about Osho and his religionless religion. His concepts of commune life, where he discouraged marriage and having children, was in a strange sense his way of saving the world. There is a lot more to his story; Swami Google can help if you are interested.

It would be remiss of me not to mention a few more Australian performers of the seventies. Acts like Brian Cadd, Sherbet, Air Supply, John Farnham, Stevie Wright, Little River Band,

Skyhooks, Daddy Cool, Billy Thorpe, Normie Rowe, Johnny O'Keefe, Dragon and Split Enz (New Zealand), and Helen Reddy, just to name a few. Whatever happened in the sixties sure opened the door for opportunities in the seventies.

But I was into surfing and just loved everything about it. It was a great way to help overcome my fears and develop some courage, because some of the waves and breaks that I attempted were not for the faint-hearted. Australia has some of the best surfing spots in the world, but I'm not going to name them. Do you think I'm silly?

During the seventies, Australia also had some of the best surfers in the world, including Michael Peterson, Mark Richards, Wayne (Rabbit) Bartholomew, Terry Fitzgerald, Peter Townend, and Tom Carroll. There were some wonderful surfing movies during this time, and one of my favourites would have to be *Morning of the Earth* by G. Wayne Thomas (the forces of the universe and the elements of space conjured up your being, your size, your time, your shape. You were created with all the beauty they could call, and earth, you surely are the measure of them all), mainly because of the soundtrack. What can I say? Go listen. "Tubular Swells" was groundbreaking as well.

I have to mention *Tracks*, the magazine for surfers. In fact, it has become the surfer's Bible. It was an integral part of a surfer's life. Even now, I get goosebumps just talking about it.

The greatest relief for me and many others in the seventies was the end of the Vietnam War for Australia in 1975. I was due to be called up for national service in 1974, so I didn't hesitate to vote for Gough Whitlam in 1972, when he announced that he would abolish compulsory national service if he was elected.

He also promised to immediately pull out all the Australian soldiers from Vietnam. He ran his campaign on the slogan "It's Time," and I agreed. His meaning was different from mine. He thought it was time for Labor to govern. I thought it was time to end the war, and I wasn't on my own.

Apart from that, it was an uneventful decade compared to the fiery sixties. There was the Patricia Hearst incident, and the IRA was bombing the Brits. Nixon resigned from office following the Watergate scandal, the only president of the United States to ever do so. There were three presidents and a presidential candidate, Nixon ('74), Ford (twice in '75), Carter ('79), and Wallace ('72), who were all the victims of an assassination attempt in the seventies. The fact that they all survived meant that assassins were getting worse or the praetorian guard was getting better. It makes one wonder sometimes about the madness around us. Here we have elected representatives of the people trying to do the right thing for the people, and someone wants to kill them. It doesn't matter if the assassin works on his own or with a sinister organisation; the question remains, what type of people are we dealing with, and what programme have they got running?

I know I'm sounding a little naïve again, but are we going to sit back and become immune to this sort of behaviour? Is it going to become an acceptable part of society? Are your children or grandchildren going to become assassins or be assassinated? What system are we going to put in place to avoid this acceptance of the unacceptable? The system in place now sure ain't working, and it never will.

Chapter 15

I got married in 1974, the same year I became a father, and the same year I stopped wetting the bed. I was living in Melbourne at the time with my in-laws. I was a thousand miles from home and couldn't wait for the right time to move back to my beloved Queensland and her warmer climate. I did enjoy my sixteen months in Melbourne, though, because of the surf spots nearby. I surfed at the famous Bells Beach on the Great Ocean Road and others such as Torquay, Gunnamatta, and Flynns and Woolamai on Phillip Island. Yes, I did see the fairy penguins. There was a supposedly secret place called the Pines, which didn't catch a swell very often, but I got it one day when it was pumping.

I've done a bit of research on why children wet the bed, but I didn't feel that any of the diagnosis matched my case, as I was still doing it at twenty years of age. I thought my problem was more psychological, as I had a lot of fear, and I was very nervy as a child. I did read somewhere, in a very blunt explanation, that bed-wetting can be caused by the fear of one's father. I thought this was interesting, and I didn't write it off, but I was more interested in a cure, not the cause.

While in Melbourne, my in-laws suggested that I see a guy in the city who might be able to help with my bed-wetting.

I didn't hesitate and was happy to try something, anything. I came home with a solid rubber mat about two and a half feet square, with wires hanging off it. I had to lay it out under the sheet on my side of the bed and plug it into a 240 volt socket. The mat was sensitive to moisture, and an alarm would go off when it got wet. I was thinking to myself that 240 volts would stop anyone from wetting the bed. I could only assume that it had a built-in transformer, but I was still nervous and desperate.

That wasn't all, people, so wait; there's more. If or when I wet the bed and the alarm went off, I'd have to first turn it off, change the sheets and my pyjamas, and then sit down and write out fifty times, "When I wake up, I must get up." The repetitive writing was almost as bad as wetting the bed. I had to do this for a week, and in that time, I wet the bed three out of seven nights. I wasn't feeling very confident that I was cured when I returned his mat. He sat me down and asked how many times I'd wet the bed in the week.

He didn't seem interested in my answer, and then he said to me, "Go home, you're cured."

I've never wet the bed since.

The last thing I ever wanted to do was get married, but an accidental pregnancy put an end to that notion. Our relationship, Jenny's and mine, seemed strained most of the time, and I felt that there were going to be challenging times ahead. I think there was a co-dependency thing happening, and I just couldn't shake her loose. I liked her most times but wasn't in love with her. That, of course, made her even more insecure. I had to live with her faults but wasn't allowed to have any of my own.

They were difficult times, and I felt my freedom had been taken away, cut down before my prime, I used to think. I resigned myself to the fact that I had a responsibility and that I had to do the best I could with the limited skills I had.

We separated in 1978 and divorced soon after. It was crazy to think that this marriage was going to last, and once an intellectual woman like her realised this, she was gone. It was five and a half years of emotional turmoil and unimaginable suffering, and I resented her for a long time afterwards, twenty-five years, to be exact.

This overview of my first marriage is a true indication of how I felt at the time. The mindset that I had was a product of my programming, my blueprint, and I had no control over the situation, no matter how hard I tried, and worse was yet to come. She was an extraordinary woman, and I do wish sometimes that I was in a better place.

She moved in with an old flame, and I soon found a girlfriend to spend time with, a girl named Lucy, I was later to marry. Things got very difficult for our daughter Chloe; she couldn't deal with this setup at all. I made the difficult decision not to see my daughter again and allowed this new couple to adopt her when they married. It turned out to be the worst decision that I have ever made.

I remarried two years later at the age of twenty-six. I know. I know. Lucy asked me to, and there was no reason not to. I have nothing against the institution of marriage, and maturity will always give one a better perspective on how society works. I think I resigned myself to the fact that this is how it is meant to be, so get on with it. It was also a great distraction from my other obvious issues.

It was tough, damn tough, not having any money and having to go into debt to pay for the wedding. But I was driven, not knowing what by, and I had an instinct for survival that would ensure a secure future. It's so easy to get caught up in the belief that if one doesn't have money, then one is poor or not very well off. I learnt during this period that where I was going was a hell of a lot better than where I'd been, and my financial situation was not a concern. This was the beginning of a new story, a new phase, a new adventure, and what felt like a new life; if you don't knock on the door, no one will open it.

It was a rocky start to what turned out to be a twenty-two-year marriage. At our wedding reception, I was caught up in an unusual incident. I knew Lucy's best friend liked me but didn't know that she was in love with me. I was standing against the wall just outside the kitchen when this friend of ours, my new wife's best friend, approached. She congratulated me and then proceeded to give me a long, passionate kiss on the lips; she then walked off, never to be seen again. The grandparents and others were looking on, and I felt very uncomfortable, not to mention embarrassed. I was left standing there wishing it had never happened. I was looking for a rewind button so that I could erase the whole incident.

I'm not sure if Lucy noticed, but she soon approached me with the question, "What was that all about? How could you do that in front of my grandparents? They were horrified."

I was not in the good books for the rest of the evening (or the next day, for that matter).

I don't think Lucy ever trusted me after that wedding night incident, even though I was just an innocent bystander. I can't help it if I'm cute.

I mustn't leave you people with the wrong impression. I was very fortunate to have been married to two extraordinary women. We were very young and all had our own programmes to deal with. We were doing our best with the limited experience, knowledge, and wisdom we had. If we'd all known more of the truth of who we were, then the relationships would have been more compatible, or maybe there wouldn't have been a relationship at all. Insecurities and low self-esteem will always distort the truth around love and trust. Where there is low self-esteem, there is little love and even less trust.

You could not have convinced me that I was doing anything wrong or that it was any fault of mine that these relationships didn't work out. One could also say that the relationships did work out because we all learnt from them.

A year or so into the marriage, we decided to have a family, which proved to be a little difficult, as I had a very low sperm count. It goes on and on, doesn't it? I'd already fathered a child, so how could this be possible? You're thinking what I thought, aren't you? I was still in resentment mode, so this doctor better have an explanation, and he did, so all was well. Phew. The doctor reassured me that a minor operation could fix the problem, and it did. Phew.

I'm going to race through the next twenty years of this story because I have a book to write and don't want to get bogged down with trivial events, when my only purpose is to save the world, which seems a long way from where we are at the moment.

I must say, though, that I'm starting to get an interesting perspective of myself from a vantage point not occupied before. There are some things coming to the surface that I'd never thought I'd reveal. It feels a bit liberating, and it's helping me to see things a little clearer. I'm not liking everything I see, but there is a light being shone on my past behaviours that allows me the opportunity to reflect, dissect, and even reminisce. To be honest, this hasn't been easy, and I'm often left depressed and even disillusioned.

I now see, though, how writing out my story can indeed give a better understanding of who I am and how I got to this point in my life. I'm beginning to think that it won't matter if nobody else reads this book; it's all been for my purpose anyway. I can't help thinking, either, that there is something deeper going on here that isn't resonating with me just yet.

Chapter 16

The next twenty or so years got under way, and it was hectic, to say the least. I started my own business; we built a house, had a second child, and built a factory; and I decided it was time to see my firstborn, eleven years since I'd last seen her. She would be almost sixteen years old. I may (or may not) discuss this meeting later on.

In mid-1994, the four of us went on a trip overseas. Two adults and two children, twelve and nine years, set upon an unsuspecting USA. You can watch all the American movies and television shows you want, but nothing prepares you to actually being there.

"You got an accent; where you from?"

"Man, you the one with the accent. I'm from Australia; how you doin'?"

It was the trip of a lifetime, and the first place we stayed was the Hotel California in San Francisco. We visited Alcatraz, crossed the Golden Gate to Sausalito, and walked through Muir Woods and its redwood forest. We dined at Pier 39 at Fisherman's Wharf. After three days, we drove south to Los Angeles, stopping at Monterey and then through Big Sur onto

Solvang. Our next stop was Disneyland. I'm not much into car parks, but the size of the Disney car park was mind-boggling. It would have been quicker to walk from the motel than the far end of the car park. Thankfully, they had people carriers running back and forth. We also stayed in San Diego with a short visit to Old Town Tijuana. Sea World and the famous San Diego Zoo were on the agenda too, and they didn't disappoint. The first animal we saw at the zoo was a koala. That's not funny, America.

The last week of our stay was in Hawaii on the island of Oahu. I got to visit the famous North Shore with Waimea Bay and, of course, Pipeline. It was June, and there's never much surf that time of the year in Hawaii, so I wasn't disappointed that it was flat.

America was a culture shock for me because everything over there was so big. The meals, the theme parks, the shopping centres, the freeways were all big. I was driving through the middle of Oahu, looking at a map and trying to find the freeway I thought we should be on. It was underneath us. We were driving on a freeway which was on top of another freeway. Have I got that wrong, people?

I went back ten years later, and something I noticed the first time was also prevalent the second time. With all due respect to the American people, and this is only an observation of a few, but I thought they were a little naïve to what is happening in the rest of the world, and that they also put a lot of faith and trust in their government. I got the impression that they believed they were a bulletproof superpower that were the envy of the rest of the world. I thought that this ignorance would make them vulnerable and underprepared if there were tough times ahead. It's just an observation, people. God bless America.

Chapter 17

The business had a lot of ups and downs over the years, and it was during the mid-to-late-nineties recession that we had to sell our home and the factory just to stay afloat. All during this time and beyond, I was heavily involved in sport administration and coaching. I was also still playing cricket on the weekend and a bit of golf during the week. I'd thrown myself into rebuilding the business and at the same time stayed very heavily involved in coaching and administration. My children had spent all their lives without much quality time with their father, and this neglect was a constant source of frustration for all.

I was on a mission, and nothing was going to get in my way or stop me until I had achieved my goal. I was obsessed with building up the business so as to sell it or to close it down when the lease was up. I believed that once I had achieved this, I could take time off to spend with my family. I stayed involved in coaching and administration, as I thought there might be full-time employment in these areas in the near future.

A friend said to me one day that I was burning the candle at both ends, but I had to believe that it was short-term pain for long-term gain. I was fading fast, physically, mentally, and emotionally, but I kept going. My depression was severe, and

I was suffering from chronic fatigue, but I dragged myself out of bed every morning, put a smile on my face, and worked for as long as I could, and did as much as I could before my mind shut down. I would have to sleep every afternoon to reenergise because I'd have a coaching session later on or a meeting in the evening. It was getting up to four meetings a week, but I had to keep going. I wanted it all to be over, but I couldn't dwell on the negative till I'd achieved my goal.

When I look back now, I can see the senselessness of it all. My programme had set in, and I'd lost control. It was like I was addicted to stress, and the more I had, the harder I fought. I was playing off the tiger tees, facing new ball bouncers, and attempted aces from a Wilson Tempest. Quitting or failing were not options, and even though I was wilting, I could always find a little more. I kept telling myself it was for the best, for a better future for all of us.

In the year 2000, we were able to buy a house, as business had picked up, and the next two years became boom years for us. But the strain was starting to tell, and the marriage wasn't going too well. We decided to put the house on the market and see where we were at when it sold. It didn't take long, and a week before settlement, Lucy informed me that she had rented a little place for her and our youngest, as the eldest had already left home.

She left while I was going through the most tumultuous period of my life. If the truth be known, though, I left her long before she left me, and I was struggling to get back to her. She did well to put up with me for so long.

I settled into a townhouse on a six-month lease. It was a hectic time, and I remember sitting down after dinner on my first night there; it felt like the weight of the world had been lifted from my shoulders. I felt at that moment that our marriage was over.

It was only a few days later that I received word that we had a buyer for our business, and it would settle sixty days later. In the matter of a couple of weeks, I'd celebrated my forty-eighth birthday, sold a business, sold a house, and separated from Lucy. The sacrificial lamb was not a sweet taste.

Once the realisation of these events had set in, I decided that my health needed attending to. I worked for the buyer of my business for a transitional period of six months, then only part time after that for a short period.

In early December 2002, a friend asked if I would do some maintenance work in a house that he'd recently bought and was now renovating. I walked into the home, with its freshly painted walls and new carpet, and immediately asked him what he was going to do with the house, as I would like to rent it. My lease was almost up on the townhouse, and places like his didn't come along every day. There was something about the house that appealed to me, but I just couldn't put my finger on it. It's hard to explain, people, and difficult to understand, but I felt me being there was no accident. It felt like there was some external, invisible force that wanted this to be my new home.

My friend informed me that he had someone looking to buy it, so he would let me know in a week. The sale fell through, and I moved in two weeks later, and little did I know that my life was about to change forever.

Chapter 18

I'm getting closer to that part of the book that concerns me. It will be about the experience I had in this house six weeks after moving in. It concerns me because I'm not sure if I have enough genius in the art of literature to find the words to describe the indescribable.

It may be best to go back three and a half years, to mid-1999, when I believe it all began. It was a time when the business wasn't doing too well. I had gotten used to the ups and downs within my chosen field and never lost faith that things would always get better. There were times when my faith wilted, but it never died. I had an employee I felt was doing the wrong thing by me, and as it turned out, he was embezzling funds on a weekly basis. Because of his knowledge of computers, I entrusted him to do my bookwork and weekly wages until I found a more appropriate person.

Upon my suspicion, I decided to advertise for a receptionist/bookkeeper and informed John that his temporary position was being replaced by a more permanent and experienced person and that I would like him to help this person through a transitional stage.

I interviewed three women, and the choice was a lot easier than I expected. The lady I chose did not sell herself very well, but she was more experienced than the others. There was something about her that was different, but I just couldn't put my finger on it. It's hard to explain, people, and difficult to understand, but I felt her being there was no accident. It felt like there was some external, invisible force that wanted her to be my new bookkeeper. I do believe you have read those words recently.

There are turning points in our lives or what one could also call defining moments, which most times are not realised until much later, after the event. This turned out to be one of those times, which I did not realise until years later. When I look back now, from my elevated vantage point, I see it as like a divine intervention, or maybe it was the return of the whisper. In fact, knowing what I know now, I don't believe the whisper ever left me.

Her name was Katherine, but I quickly gave her the nickname of Kat (which she never appreciated). The transition period was brief for obvious reasons, and John never came back after the first day of her being there. The proof of his guilt was there in black and white, and his crime was soon to be in the hands of the appropriate law enforcement.

Kat was to help lead the business out of the doldrums and into a position of great strength. I gave her the freedom to do things her way, as I had enormous faith in her abilities. This didn't go down too well with all the staff, but I had a business to run, not a kindergarten. There were times when I felt that I was working for her, and not the other way around. It certainly didn't bother me to feel like that, as I needed a lot of guidance through some very tough times.

Not long into Kat's employ, she devised a method to help build morale. After learning everyone's birthdates, she would give them all a copy of Jonathan Cainer's daily horoscopes. It wasn't long before everyone started to look forward to their daily readings, even if some pretended they weren't interested. They were always a great talking point, especially when we shared them with one another.

Below is an example of mine for today, Tuesday, December 3, 2013. "Cancer: The whole world is now slowly embarking on what some people have described as 'a consciousness revolution.' We are, collectively and individually, becoming more aware. We are starting to recognise the hidden consequences of our actions and our choices. We are growing less inclined to live in a state of ignorance and denial. All of that is most definitely happening to you at the moment. It isn't always an easy process to go through. It involves facing truths that you may prefer not to have to see. But it is doing you such good!"

Kat had some idiosyncrasies that some could not get used to. She was angrily honest and would not deal with fools lightly. Her behaviour at times was a little strange, but it never interfered with her work. She was hard working and loyal, dedicated to the cause, almost obsessed, as if it was her mission to help me achieve my goal.

I had a credit card that I used when the family went to America, and I asked Kat one day if she would be able to get it cancelled for me. It turned out to be one of the most frustrating and exasperating exercises of her career. It took months until she finally got onto the national manager who, after being threatened by an irate Leo, finally cancelled it. It was only a couple of weeks later when an unsuspecting representative of this credit card company popped in for a routine visit.

All I heard from the front reception was screams of "Get out, out, out, out, go."

She came into my office, flustered and fuming.

"Take a few deep breaths," I said.

She didn't explain till later what had happened and could only say, "The nerve."

Katherine, as she preferred to be called, had this habit of placing the palms of her hands flat on my upper back for several minutes. I was a little embarrassed at first but soon got used to it, not only because it was a regular occurrence, but it also felt really good. Whenever she sensed I was stressed or angry, she'd come in at great speed and stand behind me, performing this ritual until I'd calmed down, which didn't take long once her hands settled on my back. I could feel heat or energy coming from her palms, and it felt very relaxing. She was a strange one, and at times, she had the rest of the staff shaking their heads.

Kat's daily horoscopes, for me anyway, started to become more interesting, as the accuracy and consistency of them was uncanny. It wasn't until there was some kind of coincidence, or at least what was actually happening around me was starting to run parallel, that I started to sit up and take notice.

It's not that I ran my life and my business around these horoscopes; it was just ironic that they almost mirrored one another. It wasn't until the same message started to come through consistently that I wondered what was around the corner and was my goal nearly reached.

I wasn't that naïve to think that a daily horoscope was going to change my world for the better, but it was an interesting and harmless piece of fun that kept me in a positive frame of mind. I would joke at times with the staff when I'd tell them that my horoscope says that I should be sacking someone today. The response would always be, "Pick me, pick me."

Two years went by, and the business was prospering, and the daily horoscopes kept coming. The business had been on the market for several years but rarely attracted any interest. I decided that if it hadn't sold by the time the new lease was due in twelve months, then I would close it down. I figured I could almost make the money in the next twelve months that I would get for selling it.

Kat kept passing these horoscopes to me every day. Sometimes, I'd read them straight away, and other times, I'd put them aside to read later. Either way, they'd end up in the bin. A pattern started to emerge where the readings were informing of a huge change that would take place sometime in the future. Every second day would say the same thing in different words. Prepare for a major event, or a monumental change, or something big is on the way.

These predictions went on for the whole year, right up until Lucy and I sold our house and split up. This must have been the monumental change, but the predictions were still coming. When the buyer of the business appeared and the deal was done, I realised that this must have been the major event Jonathan was referring to. But still the predictions kept coming. "If you think the current events were big, you haven't seen anything yet," he wrote.

Kat was not comfortable with the new owners and decided not only to resign but to move to another town about four hours away. She offered to come back every three months to help with my personal quarterly tax assessments, which was a requirement of the Australian Tax Office. She would stay with me, and I would fund her trip, which would take six hours by buses and trains.

The three years she spent working for me was a roller-coaster ride, and I think in the end, she was burnt out and did not have the energy or patience to deal with a different employer. My position was that of great relief, and I found myself there because of her hard work and extraordinary dedication. I totally understood where she was at, and both of us were about to embark on a future that was uncertain.

By the time the three months had come around, I'd let go of all horoscopes and never gave Jonathan another thought. However, in the back of my mind, there was always the thought of a massive event to take place sometime in the future.

Kat's visit was very short, and it was great to see her again. We were the same age, and it is always easier to get on with someone from the same generation. She was still a little unusual, but I always seemed to attract that type. I was not physically attracted to her, but I will be forever appreciative of what she did for me. It would be another four months before I saw her again, after I moved into the house that I rented from my friend.

Chapter 19

It was early February 2003 when I picked Kat up from the train station. The tax office gives us a month's reprieve to do our tax for the December quarter, due to Xmas holidays. This suited me fine, as January was a little hectic, since I'd just moved house.

It was the same old Kat, very business-like, easy to talk to, and hard to get to know. It was Saturday, and we had a great day, even though I felt that she was always hiding something. I cooked dinner that evening, and we shared a bottle of wine, although Kat didn't drink much. There was nothing strange about this evening. She had an early night, as it was a long trip home the next day.

I had a great night's sleep and woke up a little earlier than I normally would. I also felt different, very different, as I would usually still be a bit sleepy, and a bit cranky, but I found myself very joyous and happy, almost blissful. I lay in bed for a while, but the euphoria was becoming too much to deal with, so I had to get up and wander around. I had always been able to control my happy emotions; I never wanted to get too high, as I was aware of the low times that would normally follow.

I walked down the hall to Kat's bedroom and stood in the doorway. She sat up and asked if there was anything wrong. I told her that I was feeling euphoric, and it was overwhelming me. I've never experienced anything like this before, and I don't know whether to laugh or cry. She raced over to me just as I placed my back against the hallway wall. I slid slowly down the wall till I was sitting on the floor. She sat with me and said it would be alright, just to go with it.

As I sat there, my arms started to rise up until they got to a horizontal position. This was a natural high that I'd never experienced, never thought possible, never thought existed. It was nothing like being stoned or drunk, and I'd experienced both these.

As I sat there, I slowly turned my head towards the end of the hall towards my bedroom and focused on the window within. With my arms seemingly locked in the flying position, I felt myself drift off through the earth's spheres and into the universe beyond. I was floating through an endless sky, with all matter of objects passing by. There were planets like huge balloons and giant boulders of all shapes and sizes drifting slowly by. I remember thinking; *I hope I don't get hit by one of these things.*

I felt weightless and free, fully conscious of where I was on one level; that is, I was sitting on my hallway floor with Kat, but I felt myself going deeper and deeper into space and getting closer to a point of seemingly no return. There was no sun, but there was light, and subtle colours like a mirror ball from a disco reflecting coloured light off all the floating objects. Everything seemed holographic, even me. It was the most beautiful feeling, and a large part of me just wanted to keep floating farther and farther into space.

I said to Kat, "If I keep going, I don't think I can come back."

She panicked and begged me to come back, then ordered me to get back now. Something she then said has stuck with me ever since: "James, I have not seen anyone go that far. I don't know how to deal with it, so come back."

I think I was more frightened for her at this stage, so I slowly brought my attention back to her and said, "You wouldn't believe what I've just experienced."

"I'd call it a Kundalini awakening," Kat replied.

"A what?" I enquired in my dazed state.

"Never mind," she said.

I didn't totally come back to what I'd call a normal state of consciousness; I couldn't, so I went and sat at the dining table as she prepared to have a shower. I was experiencing an altered state I had no control over.

Suddenly, Kat came running down the hallway towards me with a warning: "You'll probably have an outburst of emotion."

Before she could even finish saying those words, I burst into tears and wept uncontrollably. I put my hands up to my face and forced myself to stop crying, as I felt ridiculous.

"I'm okay now," I said.

She went off to have her shower.

This altered state stayed with me all day. I was literally spaced out the whole time. It didn't stop me from sticking to my daily routine, although it was Sunday and there wasn't much to do anyway. There wasn't any in-depth conversation with Kat, only some small talk, and no discussions on what had happened. Everything was just so surreal. My biggest chore was to drop Kat to the train station.

As we said our goodbyes, she asked, "Will you be alright to get back home?"

"I'll be fine," I replied. I only lived two minutes down the road.

This home was my sanctuary, and I was feeling very comfortable in it. The experience I had on that Sunday morning was just a prelude to what happened the very next evening. I've never forgotten the enormity of the occasion; it has stayed with me every day since.

The Monday following was a normal day, and the spaced-out feeling had left during the evening prior. There was no reason for me to think that it would happen again, and I was feeling confident that it was just a one-off. I was eager, though, to ask Kat how she knew I was going to burst into tears. That was puzzling me. I also wanted to know why it happened, but at the same time, there was no urgency, as if I knew all would be revealed in due course.

Are you with me, people? You're not falling asleep, are you? There have been many times over the years when I'd wish that it would just happen to someone else, or even many people, just so I don't get looked upon as a fruit loop or a nut case. If you have found that which you have just been informed to be a little far-fetched, then you are going to have great difficulty with the next. I don't have to justify myself to anyone anymore, and if you don't believe what you are about to read, then it will be at your detriment, not mine. I will understand the great doubt that you will have, but all I ask is that you do some research before you disregard it altogether. Even I had to research it, as I didn't understand what had happened to me. All I know is it was real.

It was about seven o'clock on the Monday evening following, and I was sitting at my desk in my office, checking emails. The office was just inside the front door and opened onto the lounge room on the right and the dining room on the left. As the office door was on a 45 degree angle, it faced the kitchen area. None of this is relevant to the story; I just wanted to paint a picture for you.

I arose from the office chair to begin preparing dinner. As I walked through the door, I was compelled to step to the right towards the front door, whereas after one step, I stopped. I stood for a few seconds and was suddenly overcome by a strange and powerful energy force. I found myself engulfed in a bright light, a powerful light that was not hot, nor was it blinding, and it spread right across the lounge room in front of me. It was white, bright, and like nothing I'd ever seen or experienced. I started to feel an overwhelming power within myself, a power that was beyond everything, an unimaginable force or energy that was incomprehensible.

It too soon engulfed me, and I felt my hands become energised with this enormous power. I raised my hands to see this white light illuminating around them, then suddenly I noticed that I was wearing a long white gown with long sleeves. I looked down, and as I leant forward, the bottom of my gown moved to expose my feet, which were adorned by beaten leather sandals that looked about two thousand years old. I noticed that my hair was lapping my shoulders, and I remember thinking, *That's not my hair* (you know how sensitive I am about my hair). As I stood still and powerful, with my hands out in front, I was filled with the most extraordinary love, a love that totally engulfed my whole being, the most powerful energy force imaginable.

As I stood there in bewilderment, overawed by the indescribable power in my hands, I realised that I would be able to heal anyone with any sickness, disease, or injury with just the touch of my hands. I looked towards the front door, with an overwhelming desire to walk through it and knock on all the doors in the world and offer my services. I had momentarily transformed into pure love and was experiencing the power of a divine being.

I started to feel so overwhelmed that it frightened me. As soon as this happened, it left me, but it also left an everlasting legacy. As soon as it was over, I made my way back to my office chair. The power was still in my hands, and I was left with a heightened feeling, a feeling of floating on the ceiling, and an awareness that I'd never experienced before. The love remained. The love was everything, and for the next few days, it was the only thing.

After a few minutes of soaking it all in, I rang Kat, and my first words were, "Has this got anything to do with God and Jesus?"

She replied, "It's got everything to do with God and Jesus."

"You wouldn't believe what just happened to me," I said.

As I explained away, all she kept saying, in amongst her giggles, was, "Oh yes, mmm, oh yes, yes, mmm yes, oh yes." I must have asked her a hundred questions and got a hundred replies, but no answers.

Chapter 20

Needless to say, my world had been turned upside down, as everything I thought, imagined, or believed had to be reassessed, revised, revalued, and every other "re-"that one can imagine. There were realisations and revelations coming at me so quickly and so often, that it was always wow, wow, wow. The greatest realisation, of course, was that I now knew what love was. This extraordinary discovery was to be the platform and the springboard for all future experiences and adventures. I had stepped into a self I never knew existed, never experienced before: my true self.

One of the first realisations I had was that everything we ever needed, wanted, or yearned for, we already had. We were born with all that we search a lifetime for. The search for me was over; I had been liberated from my wants and needs. There was a knowledge and wisdom in me that I was almost too embarrassed to mention. It was still in an embryo stage, and I felt it wanting to burst out upon an unsuspecting world. I now know that we are all born with these traits, and they are only to be nurtured throughout our childhood so that we are able to grow wise and responsible. Knowledge of self and the wisdom that goes with it are our birthright.

I felt that an enormous responsibility had fallen upon my shoulders, but at the same time, I was confident that I could deal with it. In fact, there was nothing that I couldn't deal with. There was this extraordinary feeling of being connected and that nothing was separate from me. It was sublime, and the enormity of it was almost overwhelming. I remember thinking how wonderful it could be if everyone felt this way. The knowledge of who I was and who we are was beginning to make sense, and it was a discovery far beyond my wildest imaginings.

I suddenly realised what all the sages and gurus and mystics of the world were trying to tell us. It gave me insights into their world that were beyond my imagination. I wondered how I was going to explain this discovery to the world, to my friends, or to my family. I could not produce any physical evidence, and there was no scientific experiment that could explain something like this. I had discovered a higher power, my higher power, which was to change everything for me, and I had this feeling that it wasn't just for me.

I never elaborated to anyone what had happened to me, only that I'd had this experience that changed my view of the world, and that I felt a strange power in my hands. Memories of my reverent whisper came flooding back to me, and it was almost like he had revealed himself to me in the most extraordinary way. I wondered if this was his ultimate goal and that I'd somehow been groomed all my life for this moment. It certainly didn't feel that way, having gone through so much emotional anguish and psychological torment. On many occasions, however, I did ask myself where I was getting the strength to cope. I always had this faith that if I hung in there long enough and kept going, then everything would be alright.

When I think back now, there have been times in my life when I thought I was being protected by someone or something. I think this is the reason I always kept an open mind about the existence of a God. I can remember the times when I almost drowned while surfing in big waves. A large wave had ripped the leg rope from my ankle, and by the time I'd made it to the beach, I was beyond exhaustion. The greatest battle in these situations is with the mind. I learnt that staying calm, even when being swamped by walls of white water, was crucial for survival. For anyone to panic in that situation with no one around would mean certain drowning.

The freakiest situation I ever found myself in was in my van; when one is sitting in the driver's seat, one's legs are less than a metre from the front of the vehicle. I was at a crossroad when I began to turn right into a one-way street. I didn't see the car coming from across the other side of the crossroad until my passenger yelled, "Look out!" If my calculations were correct, he should have ploughed into the front corner of the van and crushed me. I swerved to the left to avoid him, but again, I felt this action to be far too late. I remember looking down from my higher vantage point and saw what looked like a blur passing underneath me. I swerved back to the right and continued around the corner; I looked back to see where the other car was, but it was nowhere to be seen.

I said to my passenger very slowly, "How could he have not hit us?"

Once the initial euphoria of my epiphany had calmed, I started to read books that suddenly appeared in front of me. There were relatives and friends who suggested I read this one or that one, or said, "Here, this may interest you." I remember wondering where these books had been all my life, but they were the type of books that one had to be ready for. In fact, the people who gave me the books obviously weren't ready, so I ended up with them. I soon realised that the books weren't there to change my life but to explain my life. They were there to help nurture and grow my knowledge, increase my intuition, and enhance my wisdom and wonder.

Music started to become special to me again. I would lie on the couch and listen to my six-stacker all day. There were many days when after loading my choice of six CDs, I wouldn't move from the couch until they had all played (random, of course). I didn't realise it at the time, but this was my way of meditating, and it wasn't long before I was being given different types of meditation CDs, music that became lighter and quieter, as I did.

I suddenly started to write poetry and prose, finally expressing myself in the written word. I was sitting on my couch one evening not long after my experience, and I was suddenly inundated with these deep thoughts, feelings, and emotions. I couldn't stand it any longer and almost ran to the computer and started to write. Below are my first-ever lines, which eventually became a poem called *The Singer.*

"This is not to the one I love, or to those I love or love me. This is coming from within; this is coming from me. I wish you could feel the way I feel, experience what I experience, see what I see, love yourself like I love me.'

I know this isn't getting the world saved at the moment, people, but bear with me a bit longer, please. There is no small print in this book, but if you want to start reading between the lines, then be my guest. It was up to me now to dive into the pit of slime and sludge and clean it up, once and for all. I can only suggest that you come with me to learn how it's done.

I had built my life and my world around and through the eyes of a timid, fearful, shy, and worthless child who lacked courage and conviction. I had suddenly become something more special than one could ever imagine. I felt blessed with an overwhelming debt of gratitude and was compelled to do something in return. When I look at the world from my cosmic grandeur, I see everything, and when you know your self, you know everything.

Chapter 21

Although one may describe that magical moment, massive moment, magnificent moment, mystical moment, or mighty moment as a religious experience, it did not seem that way to me. I was never a religious person, and the MM, if I can abbreviate it, did not make me any more religious or the slightest bit interested in following God or joining a church. However, the MM did throw a light on another side of life that was all new to me. I always refer to the MM as a spiritual experience like no other. And by the way, it didn't take long for me to think of Jonathan Cainer and his massive prediction. I did wonder, however, what all the other Cancerians experienced.

I'd always thought that religion and spirituality went hand in hand, and religious people would have one believe that this is true, and in a lot of ways, it is. However, I believe that the true practise of spirituality is far removed from the following of religion. This discussion could go on forever, so I'd just like to say that I appreciate, understand, and accept that we all follow a chosen path (or a path chosen). This book is about a path that I'm beginning to believe was chosen for me.

There were so many changes taking place within, and as I said before, the revelations kept coming. About a week or so after my MM, I was standing by the sliding glass door in the dining room. The sun had just set behind Trombone Mountain in the distance when a mass of light appeared to engulf the fixed glass panel opposite the sliding door. I didn't take a lot of notice, as I thought it was just sunlight reflecting from somewhere, but I wasn't sure where from. Suddenly, I was overwhelmed with a revelation.

Before I go on, I will attempt to explain to you what actually happens when I experience a revelation. They are unexpected and without warning. They are profound, definite, and true. It feels like time is standing still, and it seems like they are over in a split-second. I become trance-like, with a clear mind which allows all the information to channel quickly and precisely with no doubt, fear, or anxiety. They are a pleasant experience and leave me relaxed and at peace. The message this evening was swift; I was informed that I would never fall in love again. Sadness immediately came over me, which quickly abated when I felt a strength and a power emerge. I then felt a calm, as the meaning of the message was understood.

It became clear to me that being love and being in love were two totally different things, in that I realised that I *was* love and therefore always in a place of love. I didn't need to be in love with someone to feel whole or to feel loved. I loved myself. This certainly didn't mean that I couldn't love anyone; on the contrary, it is always about loving everyone.

One of the most incredible tools that the MM left me with was the ability to deal with past traumas that were unknowingly and subconsciously holding me back from personal growth. I never knew what personal growth was until my MM. It left me with a self-belief that I never thought possible and that spelt danger for my programme. The pit of slime and sludge was on a wanted "dead only" list.

I took myself back to that beautiful child I thought was ugly and unworthy. When my brother's punches hit the side of my head, I felt my whole world cave in. Could it be that I was getting what I thought I deserved? I didn't understand the situation and could only react according to my inbuilt programme. This was a man who had his own programme running, an intoxicated, frightened, insecure man who had no control over his actions. He was still a kid himself, a kid who had no right to fight in a war, a kid who had been brainwashed to kill, against his will.

I had some guilt and shame around this event and others that I needed to express, and as writing became my way of releasing suppressed emotions, I needed to write about the experiences.

This Is War (April 2003)

Her lips were so soft, and they tasted so sweet. We must have kissed for hours. It was so exciting, so magical, so forbidden, and in broad daylight. I often wonder if they saw us, if he saw us. It was as if we didn't care if they did. It was a cricket match, of course, and I was twelfth man, of course, so I had to find something to occupy my time, of course. She was obviously bored, and we hit it off straight away. I was only sixteen, she, about eighteen, maybe nineteen. He never treated her very well, and I never liked the disrespect he showed her. He had been to the Vietnam War, so I guess he felt he didn't have to be nice to anybody. There are two things I hate, and that's war and feeling hate, but I hate war. When my brother was called up for army duties, it sent shock waves through our household. Just because he's going into the army doesn't mean he's going to war, my father reassured my mother. I knew he'd end up in Vietnam, and you couldn't fool Mum, either. After twelve months training, or what I call brainwashing, it was as if he wanted to go. The mateship, camaraderie, the sense of adventure, was all too much to resist. My brother was a beautiful man, kind-hearted, quiet, a very hard worker, and very respected in the family of eight kids. He was the second eldest, and I, second youngest.

Although he was never in the front line, and therefore, never in danger, he was still in the middle of a war. We wanted him home and we wanted him home safe. I was at high school at the time, and you know, I have no idea what the other kids were doing. Mum was a tower of strength, but you knew she was eaten up inside. There wasn't a day go by that I didn't think of my brother.

We all supported each other, which was great; after all, life must go on. She was so carefree and independent, even had her own car. How amazing was that? This lady was paying me so much attention and actually liked me. I could feel it. We were sitting in the front of the car, not sure if it was his or hers, but who cares? It just sort of happened. I couldn't believe it, and it was like heaven, front-seat heaven. Did I say we must have kissed for hours, checking every now and then to see if anyone was looking? The thrill, excitement, childishness; it was fantastic.

As the months dragged on, I was starting to wonder what he looked like. We received letters and photographs of him and army mates with some Saigon ladies. I really thought he'd found a girlfriend and was going to bring her home. The ship was to arrive on a school day, so I wasn't able to meet it with my parents. That wasn't the real reason. There wouldn't have been enough room in the car for ten people, so Mum, Dad, and my eldest brother went. The four of them were close, and they were the only ones old enough to drink.

That would have to have been the longest day in my life. The day started off so exciting, almost as exciting as that first kiss. I can't recall my mother ever being so happy, and I was as happy for her as we all were for each other. School went so slow that day, and when I got home to wait, time seemed to stand still. I heard the car pull up, and I felt myself running around in circles. *Get it together, kid*, I thought, *you're almost fifteen; find somewhere to stand and stand still; savour the moment.* I heard them all coming up the side of the shed, merry as, so glad they all made it home safe. Here he came, in full uniform, staggering a little, smiling at me as he got closer.

"You've grown," he said, as the punches came.

Are these tears I'm holding back, tears of happiness, sadness, or the pain from his fist? I can't remember who dragged him off, nor did I care. I'd just felt a knife through my heart. He's drunk, he's just got home from the war, and he can't believe how much you've grown. These are pretty good reasons, so I'll accept them, for now. I didn't speak to him much after that, nor have much to do with him. He wasn't the brother I waved goodbye to twelve or so months earlier, and I wasn't the same kid, either. Not now, not ever.

How does one cope, as I cry into the keyboard? This guy should go back and get my brother, the one I adored. Where's my brother? This is very tough, as you can see; the scars are still here, still deep.

I'll move on to that young lady now, you know, the one with the gorgeous lips. Nothing was said at the end of that day; nothing has ever been said. She broke up with him a couple of days later, and I was so proud of her. She and I rendezvoused a couple of times, but the age difference and other circumstances made it impossible to continue the relationship. We both seemed to have a maturity beyond our years and handled the situation accordingly. Almost as if we needed each other at that time, for that period of time. I certainly felt no remorse, guilt, or shame, like a killing during war, a man's gotta do what a man's gotta do.

The war took its toll on my brother, not that he showed it; a soldier, you know: drink and fight. Problem was he wanted to fight the ones who loved him. It was well over twelve

months before we realised enough is enough.
He was persuaded to move out of town for a
while and give us some respite. That's what
I'm telling you, anyway. It proved to be a
turning point in all our lives. Right at this
moment, I have forgiven him, and I hope one
day very soon, I will ask him to forgive me.

I decided to write about the anguish and guilt that had built
up over the years when I hadn't seen my daughter. At the time
of my MM, she had been back in my life for almost fourteen
years, but I was still carrying a lot of baggage. This became
prevalent one day while Lucy and I were having a weekend
away. We decided to watch a movie that neither of us had
seen before. Towards the end of the movie, the good guys
were chasing the bad guys through a kindergarten, where the
children were frightened and screaming. As one good guy
picked up a small child to comfort her, I felt an overwhelming
burst of emotion. I curled myself up in the foetus position on
the floor and sobbed uncontrollably.

Lucy knew what it was about and comforted me until I felt
better. The emotional drain left me physically exhausted for
days. Although I'd like to share with you what I wrote, it is
too personal and not relevant; well, it is relevant, but you're
still not going to see it.

One day, I walked through the front door and was still
thinking about what I'd just heard on the car radio. There was
conjecture over whether a convicted child molester should
be allowed back into society with a new identity. My mind
wandered into thoughts of why anyone would do that to a
child and how difficult it would be for that child to cope. I

suddenly stopped in my tracks as I realised what I was thinking about.

Oh, my God! Oh no! That's what happened to me. How was it possible to suppress not just the emotions but also the memories for so long? The sudden realisation that I'd been carrying this burden with me all my life horrified me. I had mixed emotions about it all, but there was also a huge amount of relief as I felt the freedom of being released from a heavy load. I knew that if I could write about it and bring it all out in the open, it would be the start of understanding why it happened, and then, I could start working on the forgiveness.

This sexual abuse experience had weighed me down all my life without me ever realising it, and it was time to lighten the load. After an initial teary session, I was off to the keyboard again to let off some steam.

Write or Wrong (March 2003)

> I am looking forward to the future, as I always have, but this time, it is as a different person, or should I say same person, different attitude, and different outlook. My strengths lie in the belief I have in myself, which gives me the confidence to deal with the different issues I know I am about to face. I also have a power that has evolved from somewhere, a special gift that is very difficult to describe and only a certain few would understand. It is the most significant thing in my life at the moment, and I am desperate to understand its true purpose.

I have been pondering for months now about the inner emotions and how and why they shape our lives the way they do. As we get older, the frequency of emotional pain and anxiety subsides, but it's still possible to retain it all from years gone by, particularly from childhood and adolescence. We can hold in anger, frustration, embarrassment, humiliation, violation, and so on. Then along comes low self-esteem, self-consciousness, shyness, and rebellion.

Isn't this all part of growing up, part of life, building character, being a man? I went deep into the basement recently to retrieve a box I'd almost forgotten I'd put there. Inside the box was a picture. Let me describe it to you: a young boy snuggled up in bed safe and sound, others in their beds all around. Should he be putting his hand there? I dare not make a sound. With his penis rubbing against mine and the scrotums gently caressing; this won't take long, and it doesn't feel that bad. I hope nobody sees us, or hears us; how embarrassing. The worst part was the fingers pinching both cheeks of my bottom at the same time. I'm being rolled over now; oh no, what's next? At least the pinching has stopped. His firm, stiff penis is rubbing up and down between the cheeks of my bottom. Oh yuk, what is that warm sticky stuff all over my backside? At least he is cleaning it off. He's gone, he's gone, but tomorrow night is yet to come and come.

The picture is now hanging on the wall, in the basement. I'll bring it up one day and see what response I get. Pick yourself up off the floor; you can't read from down there. Besides, I have a question for you. Is the above story fact or fiction, true or false? If we assume it's false, then I should close right here. Okay, I know you want more, so let's assume it's true. The ramifications are many, as I mentioned earlier. Are you keeping up? Did I mention guilt, shame, confusion, sexual implications (that's another story), hate, regret, resentment, all of which create a snowball effect as we travel down this highway of life.

So how does one cope with this trauma? I thought wrapping it up in a box and burying it deep in the basement was ingenious. No wonder I breezed through life with ease, having all that ingenuity at such a young age. The event set the stage for the rest of my life, or did it? How do we know? How would things be different? How do we know that they would have been better? I didn't do anything wrong, did I?

As it turns out, the writing was an integral part of a healing process that was to be repeated many times. I soon realised that understanding and, most importantly, forgiveness were the fastest way to liberation. When I was able to find meaning and thus able to forgive, the weight was lifted.

These days, I am able to look at the traumatic events from a different vantage point. In these situations, there is always a certain amount of self-blame or an "if only" or two. The truth is, as I see it now, we were just two people craving love. There was not enough love in our lives so our subconscious minds created a situation that reflected this lack. On a human level, this type of expression is totally unacceptable, and rightly so, as there is always one who is not a willing participant. It destroys lives and leaves people devastated. However, love comes in many forms, and the subconscious mind will not discriminate. In other words, as far as the mind is concerned, our actions are justified.

My theory is that at this age, we didn't have enough sense of self to be able to make the right choices in this situation. It's a Catch-22, really, because if we had a better sense of self with an abundance of love, we would not attract a situation like this in the first place. We create our own reality through our thoughts, conscious and subconscious, and sometimes what we create is not pretty, and it always seems to be someone else's fault. I look at my experience as just that: an experience. I don't judge it anymore or feel the guilt and shame, even though I know I created it. That's hard to swallow at times, but I'm more interested in the lack of sense of self that brought me to this situation and many others. If I know that I have created everything, then I can take responsibility for it, without criticism, judgement, or blame, and thus learn from it. Blaming others and indeed oneself is not conducive to personal growth.

It has not been so easy for others over the years, and many recipients of this behaviour have struggled throughout life, even to the point of suicide. I always understood their plight and how the guilt and shame never goes away; in fact, if left to fester, it grows to unbearable proportions. The perpetrator becomes insignificant compared to the inner turmoil.

The MM left me with a true understanding of who I was and even what I was. It was clear to me that a lot of stuff from my childhood had created enormous problems throughout my life, and these issues were to be dealt with immediately upon them arising. I seemed to know exactly how to deal with anything and everything that came my way. It was a wonderful feeling, and as burdens were lifting at one end of the scale, miracles were happening at the other.

Chapter 22

More and more revelations were coming, and some of the more powerful ones were about a woman, an assassin, suicide, and being a newborn (or even reborn). I felt the feelings and emotions of a person about to suicide. I felt the peace and calm those few seconds before the end, and the trance-like state that would allow them to perform the difficult deed. It was as if they were already gone. The assassin's mind was cool, calm, and calculating and void of emotion or attachment, which makes it a lot easier to pull the trigger.

The experience of being a baby is a bit more difficult to describe. The innocence that I felt was something special; I often feel that I want that innocence back. It's like being given a fresh start, which is an obvious difficulty with all that history attached to our psyche.

I experienced the emotions and all those other fine details of a woman that occur when she is making love. This extraordinary feeling of being a woman was a moment I will always treasure. I don't know whether it was my feminine side showing herself or I was being shown the inner complexities of the opposite sex. Either way, it was a wonderful insight and a beautiful moment. I've never looked at a woman the same again, and even though I always appreciated women, I instantly acquired much, much more respect. It was also to be very helpful in my future relationships. I was a single man, remember.

With all the revelations, realisations, and visions I was having, I was inspired to write the following piece of prose (one of my favourites):

Flying High

Well, here it comes, that extraordinary feeling of peace and power. The only thing holding it back is the slow typing. The music is on, and so is the dinner, and both are beautiful. I know the dinner will be, 'cause it was made with love. The mind and the heart are clear, and both are beautiful. The energy is high, and so is the height I'm flying. It's times like these I could be or do anything I wanted. Dangerous times for those around me, as I could take them places they wouldn't want to return from: the joys of a strong mind. I can feel things I have no right to feel, know things I have no right to know. I could dance like Fred, and sing like Bing, and run like Herb. I can feel her heart skip a beat as he makes love to her with passion and purpose. I can feel her skin tingle, her toes curl, and her eyes teary. How it feels for a man, I could make her feel.

I can enter the mind of a cliff jumper or a wrist slasher or a rifle-wielding assassin. Those moments before the life enters the next life, I can feel. The sensation of a mother suckling her young is mine, and the feeling of a newborn baby on the breast for the first time. I know the pain of a beating, the guilt, the shame, anguish, and embarrassment of rape; the warm hug of a loving mother; and the pride shown by a proud father. I have felt the extraordinary experience of a woman in love. I have felt the love for a woman and the pain when it is no longer. The good, the bad, and the ugly just make me grow stronger.

Come with me if you dare; I don't really care how you fare. I'll be alright, 'cause I have the insight, the light, and the might. My heart holds the power, and my mind knows that. The mind learns and the heart feels, and the conscious is aware; I ain't going nowhere near despair. I'm in love, and I always have been, with this heart of mine. To love this heart is to love that heart, and I feel your heart feeling mine, and that is what it is all about.

Where does this mind of mine wander? What is inside my head? Am I standing on the edge of a cliff with a rifle in my hand and a razor blade in my pocket? Am I lying in my mother's arms, bobbing my head, trying to find that nipple? Am I making love to that woman who I feel I am? I hope this is not scaring anybody. Yes, I do; if you're scared, you're not with me, so get off my page. If you're enjoying the journey, then you know where I am, so stay with me, and enjoy the next moment in time.

I have more to give than one can imagine, only to be given when I'm ready, and to be given to those who are ready. Hop on my bus, my train, my plane, and let's take that road less travelled. Let's leave loads of footprints in

the sand; let's lighten the load; let's enlighten
the crowd, frighten the evil, and widen the
straight and narrow. I am flying. I am soaring.
I am cruising. I am too high for you now.

I felt like I'd become a highly evolved being; a mini version of
that powerful entity I'd experienced that seemed like some sort
of spirit with a divine and holy connection. It became evident
very quickly that a new Jimmy Dinge had emerged from
the depths of the delusion, known as our reality, to a cosmic
consciousness that was to become my world, my reality. There
was a part of me that was floating, drifting, and cruising, trying
to keep my feet on the ground, and another trying to get by in
the illusion that I'd been in all my life.

I often wonder if other people have had the same experience
as me in the last hundred years or so; even a thousand years
or so would interest me. I wonder how they coped and what
they did about it. It is with me every day and won't let go. It
felt like the Holy Spirit in physical form. It was that powerful.

One of the most difficult things was how to share the experience
or explain it to people. I'm sure if there were others, they would
have found it just as difficult as I have. I'm almost certain some
would've ended up in psychiatric wards or mental institutions. I
thought at times I was going out of my mind. In a way, I was;
I just wouldn't allow myself to go insane. It was a bit like my
teenage years when at times I was so emotionally distraught, but I
wouldn't allow thoughts of suicide to enter my mind. Those who
dealt with the experience a bit better would probably have joined
the priesthood or formed some sort of religious or spiritual cult.

I must say, though, that I have a wonderful view of the world
from where I look. I call it the look of love.

Chapter 23

Two months had gone by, and Kat was due to pay a visit. I couldn't wait for her arrival, as I still had many questions that needed answers. Why had this extraordinary thing happened to me, and what was I to do with it? I had an enormous responsibility bestowed upon me, and I needed some direction.

She was a strange woman, and it was very difficult to get any answers from her. "Don't think that you know everything, James," she said. "You have a lot of work to do on yourself. You have to do the work."

"What work?" I asked. "Why did this happen to me?"

"The universe must be in a great hurry," she replied. Kat would always reply with cryptic statements, and I never seemed to get any answers.

"Light workers," she'd say. "We need more light workers."

"So I'm a light worker, am I? What exactly does that mean?" I asked, not expecting to be enlightened, so to speak.

"The planet is in desperate need of help. It will only be through the work of spiritual people, light workers, and healers that it can be saved before it is too late, if it isn't too late already."

"Oh, shit, you're joking," I replied. "I have no idea how to go about that."

"Do the work, James. Do the work," she kept saying.

Kat went on to say that everyone had the power within to heal themselves and to heal others as well. They had everything that I had discovered: knowledge, wisdom, love, compassion, and understanding. The difference was that I'd been made aware of the truth of who I was.

Deep down, I knew that I had a huge responsibility to do something but did not know what until Kat had informed me. I didn't really want to know about it; I didn't want to do the work, and I wasn't sure what she meant by that, anyway. I was starting to have a really good time; my confidence and self-esteem were taking me places I never dreamed of. If I had not experienced the MM, I would have laughed at her for suggesting, even touching on something as outrageous as saving the planet from disaster.

I was just beginning to realise how many negative programmes and limiting beliefs I had running through my subconscious. Was this the work I was meant to do, or was there other stuff I didn't know about? I thought I knew everything. I didn't know the planet was in that much trouble, though. Such is the ignorance of us all when we are caught up in our own self-importance that we don't pay attention or even care about the troubles of the world.

At the risk of a contradiction, I wonder if we see ourselves as being important enough to play a part in the well-being of the planet.

I didn't have the nerve to tell Kat about a new relationship I had entered into, not that it was any of her business. However, I wanted to inform her of some healing work I'd been doing with a woman named Kelly, who had some long-term physical problems, and this of course was creating emotional and psychological issues. The cause of her physical problem was probably rooted in her other issues, but it was clear to me that Kelly wasn't going to get better while in her current mental state.

I wasn't into the psychological side of healing at that stage, but I was aware that they were related. The power in my hands and an inner knowing seemed enough to make a difference to someone's frame of mind. Kelly had been an acquaintance for many years, and a chance meeting led to a more intimate relationship. Three weeks into the relationship, I decided it was time. I hadn't been intimate with a woman for nine months, and as it turned out, it had been fourteen years for Kelly. It was an extraordinary experience for both of us in so many ways and for so many reasons.

For me, it was because I was a different person and one who was in touch with a side of my self that I never knew existed, till that moment. I experienced an altered state and became guided by this new sense of knowing, knowing what to do, when to do it, and how to do it. My heightened senses were at the peak of their pleasures, and to be able to experience for so long was all too new to me. The curse of the bedroom was over for me, and this was one of the most satisfying effects and what I was to deem miracles of my epiphany.

For Kelly, it was an experience she described as unbelievable, unforgettable, and amazing. Of course, I didn't let on at this stage that I'd had a revelation which allowed me to gain some insights into the secret wonders of a woman's world, her emotions, and her body.

It's probably about now, people, that we have a serious chat. You're beginning to wonder if this guy is for real. Right now, I'm putting myself in your shoes and ask that you put yourself in mine. This was not and never was an ego-driven exercise, as I'm sure most people would think, and for obvious reasons. I was still in the height of my powers, and my sense of self was far removed from the ego-driven person I'd been all my life. I was experiencing a heightened way of living, a new way of thinking, seeing, doing, being, and touching. The battle with my ego was yet to come. I'm trying to find the words here that can convince you, the people of the world, that what I experienced and am still experiencing is real. Even if it is beyond one's comprehension, come with me, come into my world. Let go of all the doubt and the fear that something is going to harm you. There is nothing to fear but fear itself; fear is just a game the mind invented to keep the ego happy. It is better to love fear than to fear love.

From the very beginning of my experience, I developed a strong inner sense of self; I was a person of high integrity who could make decisions from within a framework of parameters that would allow miracles to happen. There was always a sense that it was all part of a bigger picture and not to get carried away with the pieces of a puzzle being put together. It was still an exhilarating ride, and there was no turning back.

I had to go through a period of adjustment, whereas if I wanted to be true to myself, I had to let go of control. I wasn't in the driver's seat anymore and had to have faith that I was heading in the right direction at the right speed. I was feeling fancy-free and as relaxed as I'd ever been in my life. I let love take over and allowed the natural flow of life to take its course. This is something anyone can do, and many have, with extraordinary results.

It was Saturday night, so I cooked dinner for Kat and myself, and enjoyed it with a nice bottle of wine. Kat asked if I would like to go to a spiritual church meeting being run by a friend of hers the next day. I said yes apprehensively, knowing that I really had no choice, if you know what I mean. She also asked if I'd heard of psychometry, as she removed a ring from her finger and handed it to me. I told her that I had no idea what she was talking about.

"Hold my ring in your hand and tell me what you can about it," she said.

I laughed at her and said, "You must be joking."

"Just try it," she said. "Relax and focus on the ring."

I looked at the ring, took a deep breath, and then ran my fingers over it. "This ring is very old," I finally said.

"That's obvious," she replied.

"Okay then, it belonged to your mother, no, your grandmother; maybe both. There was something very special about your grandmother, and there is something regal about this ring. Did she know royalty?" I asked.

"That's very good, James," she replied.

"Well, tell me about the ring," I said.

"The ring was a gift to my grandmother from the king of Finland. They were close friends. I don't think there was any more to it," she informed me.

"I'm not so sure about that," I replied.

It was time to learn a bit more about Kat, so I pressed her on a few subjects, trying not to pry too much. She always seemed apprehensive when it came to talking about herself. She had been a travelling salesperson in a previous job, selling cosmetics (which, I might add, she hardly ever wore).

As she spoke, she opened up a little about some personal experiences that had helped her to grow as a person but still wouldn't elaborate too much, except that she went through a stage of drinking too much. I respected her privacy, but reading between the lines, without making judgements about her, everything started to make sense to me. It seemed like she had made some decisions in her life that she has regretted, and wasn't ready to share with anyone.

Kat had barely touched her wine, and as I held my hand out to suggest that I take it, she said, "No, it's okay; I'll finish it, but this'll do me."

She spoke of her therapy and her mentor and saviour who she said was very ill at the moment. I could sense her deep gratitude for him and her concern for his health. I got the impression that he was a religious man and that he showed her the way to God and consequently her self. Kat's obvious experience of God had taken her down a spiritual path, as I knew that she was not religious. She was inept in spiritual matters, far more than I realised. I suddenly had this feeling that she'd been my guardian angel and was now a guide to help me through this maze of mystical magic I had found myself in.

My first experience of a spiritual church was about to take place, and I had no idea what to expect. Kat introduced me to her weird friend, who asked if I was looking forward to the meeting.

Before I could answer, she quickly quipped, "You can't lie to a clairvoyant, you know."

"Then I don't have to answer the question?" I replied.

She liked me. I could tell.

It was around Easter time, so there was a visit from a local Christian priest, which I found surprising. He spoke of the crucifixion of Christ and how the soldier, upon plunging his sword into the side of Jesus, was covered in water which came spurting from the wound. I found that very interesting, as I'd never heard that story before. I wondered how much more information about Jesus that I was ignorant to.

I let that go for now and watched the remainder of the meeting with an open mind. There was a small ceremony, with moments of prayer and meditation. I watched healers place their hands on the upper backs of volunteer recipients. That looked familiar. There were clairvoyants raising their hands to offer others a reading, doing so seemingly as entertainment, although I think I was the only one entertaining it as entertainment.

As we were leaving, Kat's friend asked if I enjoyed the morning. She reminded me again that I can't lie to a clairvoyant.

We all laughed for a moment, and then I said, "Then I don't need to answer."

Maybe she didn't like me after all.

Chapter 24

This was the last time that Kat was to visit, so she gave me a quick rundown on how to do a reconciliation of my company accounts and suggested I get a bookkeeper in to check it when it's due. I was okay with that and suggested that I visit her from time to time. She said that she'd be delighted to have me.

It was probably a good thing, as Kat and I seemed to be heading in different directions, and I don't think she was ever impressed with my attitude towards my spiritual awareness or to her friends and their obvious gifts. Besides, I had to save the world, so I had a lot of work to do, and I very quickly realised that I was on my own in this search for the meaning of the MM.

Kelly and I spent time together and talked about the philosophies of life, our spiritual nature, and how we as human beings were a lot more than we ever imagined. We had to let go of everything we believed and start looking at everything in a different way, a spiritual way. I told her of my amazing experience and how it changed my whole way of thinking and being.

Not long after my MM, I had a feeling of being transient. I had never heard the word before, but it rolled off my lips so eloquently. It was if I could go anywhere in the world at the drop of a hat.

My relationship with Kelly was soon to end, which left her devastated. I explained that even though I could love her like she's never been loved before; I could never fall in love with her. My transient nature and the fact that I'd found a love within that kept me secure always made it difficult to have a long-term relationship. We remained friends and would meet up occasionally. Her spirit was free, and her health improved dramatically.

This is the reason, people, that it has taken me so long to write this story. It is so unbelievable that it must be true. I can only tell it how it was. I'm really a very humble guy and feel a bit silly at times when I try to detail some of the events. I keep reminding myself that they are important because they are small pieces of a big picture. Spiritual people will get it straight up, but I'm not here to preach to the converted. I'm aiming at the nonspiritual, the intellects, the educators, the politicians, the people who have been feeding us crap so long that there are generations who believe it to be their truth, all those who need to be informed that a large part of who they are is missing in their life right now. This planet has no chance unless you are willing to see the truth.

There is a saying by W H Auden that has resonated with me, which goes like this: "We are all here on earth to help others. What on earth the others are doing here, I don't know.'

I will continue with the rest of my story, and if I begin to lose credibility, then it will be at your peril, so give the book to somebody who cares. If I gain credibility, then I know that we have a chance of saving the world.

Sometimes, I wish I could go back ten years and walk through that front door when I had the chance. If I had been criticised or crucified, then so be it. The only thing that stopped me was fear, fear of ridicule because of my upbringing, my conditioning, my blueprint. I was a fear being who lacked courage and was afraid of criticism. I have now become a love being with wisdom, knowledge, and power, who with a little help from my friends may just be able to save this world. So please, don't get in my way.

I kept reading books which were constantly confirming that there is more to this world than meets the eye. I often wondered how people could understand these books if they didn't know what I knew, that is, hadn't experienced a MM. I soon realised that people had been studying these books for years and looked upon them as information, whereas I saw them as confirmation.

During my time with Kelly, I made contact with a friend of a friend who lived in another state. We emailed and texted from time to time, and eventually, I invited her to come up and live with me. Her name was Dianne, and we'd met briefly a couple of times over the years. She was very spiritual and had been for many years. I made that statement for your purpose, people. The fact is that we are all spiritual, always. Our spiritual nature is overshadowed when children get programmed to fit into a society that does not accept spirituality or spiritual matters. I am beginning to think that this type of deprivation is a form of child abuse.

Because of Di's transient nature, it wasn't a difficult decision for her to make. It was to be a nine-month stay with me. The territory covered was mind boggling, and we didn't even have to leave the comfort of our home. Di taught me so much about the mind/body connection and how our spirit plays a vital role in this connection. It was a roller-coaster ride of discovery, adventure, learning, teaching, and healing. Let go, she would say, let go of all that is not important, not relevant to who you are. Be more and do less, and more will be done. I discovered how powerful my subconscious was and realised that I still had so many limiting beliefs and programmes. One could say that I was beginning to see who I was not; as much as who I truly was.

I informed Di of how my MM had changed my view of the world and that I now looked out upon it without judgements, criticism, blame, or condemnation. Even the intellects were beginning to look good; I realised they had their own programmes they weren't aware of. It still didn't mean that I wasn't holding them accountable for the state of the world, whichever way you see it. Any time I was to judge was a failure of mine to be conscious of my thoughts and to allow fragments of a programme from within to rise up. This was always a sign of more work to be done.

Di informed me that whenever we judge another, we are really only judging ourselves. People are our mirror, and what we see in others is what we see in ourselves. I thought that was the most profound statement, and upon looking into it more deeply, I was astonished at how powerful it was. It was to become one of the most important pieces of knowledge for my future travels. It threw a light on what I was saying and thinking at all times.

I had an ego that didn't want to let go of certain programmes because I was comfortable with that belief, even if it held me back. At times, things were getting very tough, but I had gone too far down this road, the road less travelled, to turn back. I was told to be aware of signs, signs that would assist me along the way. I remembered what Kat would say and I could hear her voice ringing in my head: do the work, do the work. I was beginning to realise what she meant.

I was doing the work, doing the work, but only because I had no choice. It seemed as though the minute I made a decision or had an intention, it would start the ball rolling, and all I could do was fasten my seat belt and hang on. I also had no idea why I was doing the work. I felt hungry for more and more information. I think deep down, I was looking for a reason why I had experienced the MM; I wondered if there was anyone out there who had experienced it too.

I sat down with Di one day and told her that I wanted to make a commitment to her and asked if she'd be okay with that. She seemed very pleased, and we began to discuss our immediate future. Just as we started, I felt this strange sense of urgency, as if something wanted to interfere. What happened next was really weird. I felt this extraordinary energy around, with a message that came to me loud and clear. It's hard to explain, people, and difficult to understand, but I felt an invisible force that made it quite clear that this relationship was not for me. Dianne moved out a few days later.

I was again saddened by events that were seemingly, no, definitely out of my control. I stayed close friends with both Kelly and Dianne, and loved them dearly, but there was never a feeling of being in love. I had this weird feeling that I was destined for something bigger than all of us, and they were there to help me grow and develop, which they both did in the most beautiful ways.

Chapter 25

Over the next few months, I felt very hesitant about meeting another woman, and I also felt that I needed time to myself for a while. Kelly and I would still meet up on occasions, which was always a wonderful experience. I still had my cricket commitments and my Friday afternoon golf with a friend. I played the occasional social tennis with a group of friends as well. I went back to work after a twelve-month break. I felt refreshed and keen to do well for the people who had saved my life, the couple who had bought my business.

I was still writing poetry and other pieces, which I now realise was an integral part of my healing process. It was helping me to change old beliefs. I was still reading books, listening to CDs, meditating, and watching DVDs. Kelly and I would go to spiritual festivals when they were on. A lot of it was the same old stuff over and over again, but every now and then, something new and inspirational would catch my attention. After experiencing my MM, though, nothing anyone said or did came close. I often wondered what I would think of all this spiritual stuff if I hadn't had that MM. Probably the same thing you're thinking, people.

But I kept moving through this maze of mystery and magic, keeping one foot in the world I was brought up in, while being fascinated by this world of intrigue and truth. It was like having one foot in the forest and being torn between exploring it before they cut it down and retreating to the comfort of old beliefs that were hanging by their fingernails.

If I wasn't meditating, I was in front of my computer and was quickly finding out the magic of both. There was a period of a few weeks where a window would pop up on my screen, and I would just go to its top corner and hit the X. I was always too preoccupied to concern myself with how to stop this window from appearing.

Finally, one day, I dropped my hands on the desk firmly and said, "What is this? What are you trying to tell me?"

The window happened to be a dating site, which did not interest me one bit until that moment. I immediately thought to myself that this must be a sign. I could hear the angels dancing a jig. The message finally got through.

The next stage on this remarkable path to self-realisation was about to begin. I fastened my seat belt; let go of doubts, fears, and inhibitions; and prepared myself for the ride of my life. I was on a huge learning curve; my integrity would be challenged while my higher intentions were scrutinised. But it was all beyond my control, right?

I remember as a teenager, my brothers and I would play poker using matchsticks instead of money. At the end of one game, I was left with seven matchsticks. I placed them in the palm of my hand and stared at them. My mother noticed this, sat beside me, and said, "A penny for your thoughts, James."

I replied, "I'd like a girlfriend for every matchstick in my hand."

"Huh, you wouldn't know what to do with them," she quipped.

I looked up at her with a cheeky wry smile and never said a word. She looked back at me with the same cheeky wry smile, and nothing more was said. If there's a motto to that story, it's be careful what you ask for, no matter what age you are.

I read that we learn more about ourselves through the relationships we have with others, more so when they are intimate relationships. It is no accident when our holographic illusion crosses the path of another. The ensuing relationship happens so that one or both people learn something about themselves from the other. What better way to learn about oneself than through the love of a woman and the love for a woman. I always showed much love and great respect for these extraordinary people.

I cannot stress enough how important women are to the welfare of humanity. They are natural nurturers, and I believe, no, I know they are aware of a special connection to all life and to the planet. I would leave what was left of my ego at home and go deep with them and reap the rewards. Having said that, there were times when I thought I may have been on one big ego trip. The secret was in letting go and allowing the natural flow of life to unravel. Women are not silly, and they will humour one's ego only for a little while. I was in the midst of love, and love was on offer at all times. The love I speak of is that endless essence which is all of us.

From August of 2005 to Christmas 2008, I had the pleasure of having intimate relationships with seven women. I am just so thankful that I didn't have more than seven matchsticks in my hand all those years ago.

These relationships inspired me to write a lot of poetry about the deep and meaningful experiences I'd had. They were short relationships with seemingly no purpose, but they were all deep and meaningful to me. It had nothing to do with notches on belt buckles or mastering bra straps. I wasn't there for the moment of pleasure or the pretence and promises. Love brought me there, love kept me there, and love sent me away.

It's very unlikely that many of these relationships and experiences would have happened if I hadn't experienced my MM. Besides, this path I am on brought me to this book, which is one of my contributions to saving the world. It is also to bring awareness to the people of the world. This is not about what I know; this is about what you don't know.

Chapter 26

It was late in August 2005. I had just got back from seven days in Bali and was recovering from a touch of "Bali belly." I was still in adventure mode and ready for a fun time. What more could a woman want: a man who was relaxed, fun-loving, fancy-free, and cute to boot?

I said to a friend when I got back, "I don't feel normal anymore or fit in as I used to."

He replied, "I never thought you were normal from the moment we met, James."

I was a bit miffed by this statement, as we'd known each other for twenty-eight years.

Bali was a very uplifting and spiritual experience for me; I'd always been fascinated by other cultures but never came face to face with them, being a country boy and all.

My first relationship when I returned from Bali was with a schoolteacher, an intellectual. I know what you're thinking, people. What we focus on, we attract.

When I first met Eve, I decided to call her Evie. Her name reminded me of Stevie Wright's hit song "Evie." Stevie Wright was the lead singer of the Easybeats, the iconic band in the late sixties. They had a hit called "Friday on My Mind," which went down really well with us teenagers who were always looking forward to Friday arvos. I was starting to realise that I knew a little more than most about the bands and music of the sixties and seventies. I was also starting to realise that I was a little different from everyone else.

One evening while I was lying across her big blue leather couch, a revelation came to me. I said to Evie, "Did you know that we could have peace on earth in an instant?"

"Being a realist, James, I don't believe that's possible," she replied.

"Mass consciousness, Evie," I informed her.

"Yes, that would do it," she replied, "but how does one create mass consciousness?"

"Well," I said, "I'm not sure, but there may come a time when your realism and my ideology will have to compromise; mass consciousness may be the only option." I went on to say, "We will only have peace on earth when we find peace within. This has been said by many people many times, and until this ideal reality sets in, change will not happen."

That short conversation may have been the catalyst that set off a sudden impulse, a shift in my consciousness that caused me to become aware of a greater responsibility that we all had on this planet. It wasn't the first time that I'd felt oneness, but this time, it was with all humanity. What affected one, affected all.

As usual, I had to let this go and stay in the moment. No doubt, I would be summoned at a later date for further instructions.

Intellectual or not, Evie found my way of thinking intriguing and was swayed to delve deeper into my world (or should I say her world?). Her research and discoveries revealed that in fact we are dealing with another dimension, a realm that sits just beyond our consciousness, a sixth sense (or maybe even a seventh sense).

When we first met, I remember asking her if she wanted to go beyond. I was being serious and a little cheeky as well, trying to tease her intellect. She admitted later that she had no idea what the hell I was talking about, but she said yes anyway. She now knows what I meant.

Evie was easy-going, open-minded, and not very spiritual; she had an ego as big as a bus, no, a bus depot. I didn't hold back, and I think she was thankful for that. She eventually set off on a path of self-discovery and has never looked back. We had a wonderful six-month relationship, and an amicable breakup left us as very good friends.

Chapter 27

I wandered into relationships with several more women, including a dancer, a writer, and a Realtor.

I couldn't seem to settle into a long-lasting relationship. The opportunities were there, but nothing would eventuate. I was sure if the right person came along, I would commit to her.

I often wondered what was happening to me, and sometimes I'd feel guilty and not know why. I kept asking myself if anyone was being hurt or disadvantaged by what was happening. I would always be aware that whenever I made a decision, it was not to hurt anyone. I somehow knew that because I was in the midst of this powerful energy, I had to keep going. I felt like I was floating around in a higher state of consciousness, surrounded by a mighty force that would sweep anyone and everyone up that stepped inside this ring of power. It wasn't just the women, either, as all areas of my life were being influenced by the love I was feeling, being, and projecting.

I was just as happy being on my own with my books, computer, and meditation. If there are things I've learnt on this fascinating ride, it's the power of letting go and the power of now, this present moment. I just followed the prompts and went where I was guided.

After meeting Evie, I dumped the dating site for good, as I knew that it had served its purpose. Any future dating would have to be instigated by the universe. It didn't take long, as the study of self must be more urgent than time by myself.

My next relationship was with Faye; this was challenging, and there were many times during our twelve months together when I would ask myself what I was doing in this relationship. But no matter the circumstances, there was an underlying reason for being there, and I was determined to make the most of the relationship and learn from the experience. I asked myself on occasions if it would be possible for me to live with Faye and make a go of it. But there was always something within not allowing me to entertain that thought. I don't believe Faye was ready for a live-in relationship, either, but the thought crossed my mind.

At times, it was a battle to remain as an individual, which was to stay true to myself and not get drawn into her web of emotional and psychological manipulation. Her angry outbursts were not aimed at me, but it was clear they were to make me feel guilty and to pity her, which they did neither. It was her stuff, and only she could deal with it. Faye was a master manipulator, and if it wasn't for my conscious awareness of what was happening, I would have been dragged into her web and eaten alive.

This, of course, did not help the situation, as she could not maintain control over me as she would have liked. My vulnerabilities were non-existent and her tactics ineffective. But she never gave up, and over time, I could feel her slowly wearing me down. I had to believe that Faye was teaching me something about myself that I wasn't seeing with my own eyes or mind. What was she reflecting back to me? What part of me was I not seeing in her?

We had many wonderful times together during our twelve months, but there was always a consistent ruthless aggression that in the end made it too hard. Her compulsive, obsessive, and possessive behaviour was to outgrow her natural compassion, passion, and obvious love she had for me. Faye's manipulation finally wore me down; my physical, emotional, and physiological strength had waned to the point where I had to say, "If you don't leave, I will die." I was that sick, and after a month of telling Faye that the relationship had run its course, she finally left me alone.

It took me weeks to recover, with several visits to the doctor for tests and check-ups. Once I got the physical clearance, I realised that the problem was emotional and psychological, and the stress and strain of the relationship had caught up with me. I just wanted to know what the lesson was, because I was nothing like Faye and couldn't understand the relevance of the mirror.

Upon my recovery, I decided it was time to move out of the house that had served me so well. It's hard to explain, but I'd felt a shift had taken place within me, and it was time to go with it. Everything changes, nothing stays the same was a philosophy I'd taken on board many years earlier, and where once I would have feared change, I now embraced it. I now knew that change was one of the greatest ways to let go of our ego-created fears, which would clear the way for more exciting adventures and a lot of important self-development. My energy had been depleted during my relationship with Faye, and I needed time and a place to rejuvenate.

I told Evie of my plan to move, and she suggested that I stay in her spare room for a while, as she needed a roommate to help with expenses.

"How did I know you were going to say that?" I remarked.

"I knew weeks ago that you were moving in with me," she replied.

"So did I," I said.

Chapter 28

Evie lived in a townhouse; my room was one of three bedrooms upstairs. It was to be my retreat while I regained my strength. I was physically okay, emotionally well, and as sane as anyone. This was a feeling of being spiritually drained, if that's possible. My best explanation would be that I felt disconnected from my true self and needed to get back the power that I'd felt prior to my relationship with Faye. This period of self-imposed celibacy was no doubt the result of a torrid affair and maybe even the reason for someone like Faye to come into my life. I had the feeling, though, that I may have been heading in the wrong direction before Faye had come along, and there was a sense that this recovery period would take me beyond anything I had ever imagined.

I was still working full-time, but all other commitments had fallen by the wayside, which I felt was meant to be. I was heading back inside and didn't need any of the distractions that previously occupied my time and mind. Reading, writing, and meditation became a way of life for many months. Evie and I always talked about spirituality and were way beyond television soap operas and trivial issues of any kind. Her ideomotor was in full force, and it always made for interesting conversation.

Evie had discovered an amazing gift through her spiritual practice; apart from her contact with her angels, she was able to read past lives and touched on medical intuitiveness and clairvoyance. With my revelations and Evie's insights, one can understand why our conversations were interesting, even off the planet.

One Sunday evening, we visited a local Christian church and experienced a very modern and theatrical version of prayer and worship. After making a small donation, we left early, as we felt our version of God was a little different from the church. It was the same God but not the same belief. I had this deep knowing that God was good for us but religion wasn't.

As we were leaving, I informed Evie of a spiritual church that I'd heard about not far from where she lived. It was still early, so we decided to check it out. We walked in a little late but were politely welcomed as we took a seat. It was not much different from the one Kat took me to, except it was a much smaller group. There was a lady dressed in white sitting at a table, and I wondered if she was the reason I was there. There was something about her, but I just couldn't put my finger on it. You know the story. I decided that I would go back the following week, not knowing if she was single or otherwise. What am I saying? Of course she was available. That's what I was doing there.

My reverent whisper had obviously decided that my period of celibacy was to come to an end. It really didn't bother me either way, but we both knew, unbeknown to her, that this attractive lady was to be my next lover.

I didn't know what was about to hit me.

I had never met anyone like Erin before, and as you know, I'd met a few. There was definitely something about this woman, and about four weeks into the relationship, I saw another side to her. There were times when the slightest thing would send her into a frenzy of anger, criticism, and blame. I seemed to be doing something wrong all the time and felt terrible that she had been hurt. I would apologise profusely, but nothing would stop her rage. There were a lot of magic moments, but every now and then, it all turned crazy.

I would come home in a mess at times, wondering what to do or even what I had done. I thought I was going crazy and stayed away as much as I possibly could. But I was always drawn back to her, back to a beautiful loving person, until I did or said something wrong. She seemed to thrive on confrontation, and this did not match my new way of being. I didn't live far from her, so I decided that when things flared up, I would just leave. It was always my fault, so the apologies were always one way.

Erin didn't like the idea that I was living with a former lover, so I would always say, "Well, ask me to live with you."

I knew she wasn't ready for that; otherwise, I wouldn't have asked. I certainly wasn't moving out of Evie's just to appease her fears and jealousy.

I knew a teenage girl once who had her ex-boyfriend's initials tattooed on her wrist after he was killed in a car accident.

I said to her, "What if your future husband doesn't like the tattoo?"

Her response was, "Then he won't be my future husband."

Fair enough, I thought.

This twelve-month relationship with Erin was like a roller-coaster ride on steroids. My relationship with Faye was a walk in the park compared to this one. Why did I bother staying with her for so long, I hear you ask? Well, people, I was following the prompts, doing as I was guided, which is difficult for many to understand. Deep down, I knew it was the place I was meant to be, and this woman was teaching me something about myself that I didn't know. It was the same with Faye, and even though I still didn't know what that was all about, there will come a day when all will be revealed. Don't worry; you'll be the first to know.

The Sunday night church meetings were always fun, and I met so many interesting people. There would be guest speakers from time to time who would talk on different spiritual matters, which I lapped up. There were the usual clairvoyants and psychometry experts, meditation, and a bit of singing.

Erin and I would also visit a Taoist temple; the Buddha played an important role in their philosophy. The people involved were Taiwanese and were very beautiful, kind, and loving, as were all who attended. It was a humbling experience for me; the teachings, writings, and philosophies of Taoism are as close to the truth as one can get. It was an honour and a privilege to receive the Tao from several masters who were visiting from Taiwan. I received a book called *The Three Treasures of Tao*; the following is an excerpt from chapter 1:

> Today you have received the Tao which is the
> ultimate aim of existence. All of the Buddhas
> and Saints received the Tao in the past and,
> by transcending the limitations of birth and

death, have become immortal. That which you have received today is the same Tao.

Formerly, one who intended to receive the Tao had to abandon worldly possessions and enjoyments. If he was a King he had to abandon his kingdom. If he was a high official he had to resign his high position, leave his family and go to the remote mountains to seek a master who would transmit the Tao to him. After much suffering he would gradually perfect his conduct, purify his mind and heart and perform many good deeds. For his sincerity, God would send Buddha to transmit the Tao to him. Under such conditions a person able to succeed was hard to find! During that period the Tao was secretly transmitted from one Patriarch to another.

Today we need not go to the remote mountains in order to cultivate ourselves. We may find the means to do so in our own environment. Therefore we must take full advantage of our fortunate circumstances because we are in close proximity to the Tao. Why is the Tao so accessible to us at this time? It is because mankind is facing great calamities which signal the destruction of the human race.'

That last sentence reminded me of Kat when she said, "The universe must be in a hurry."

Erin was in the know, and over the twelve months with her, I met dozens of fascinating people in the spiritual world. There were so many different healing modalities, and they all believed in what they were doing. After what I'd experienced, I had no doubt in their abilities. People were healing with candles, light, crystals, drums, hypnosis, psychic surgery, Bowen therapy, reiki, shamanism, kinesiology, past life regression, and chakra balancing, to name a few. There were psychic mediums, channels, astrologers, tarot readers, energy healers, self-development gurus, spiritual guides, teachers, meditation guides, and yoga teachers. I often wondered where I fitted in with this array of spiritual allsorts. My hands and my love were all I seemed to need. It did occur to me, though, that these spiritual warriors were the light workers Kat referred to.

The first time I moved in with Erin lasted four weeks. The first three weeks were heaven, and I experienced a wonderful, loving, and caring person. I didn't mind her short and insignificant outbursts, but when they continued, I had to draw on my self-respect and tell myself I was more worthy and such treatment was unacceptable. I would tell Erin that I stood resolute in who I was, and nothing she said could change that. I felt like I was walking on eggshells at times, so I asked her where her boundaries were and suggested that she not keep moving them.

It had become apparent to me that she had multiple personalities and suffered from obsessive-compulsive disorder. One afternoon, I hung two loads of washing out for her after work. When she came home, she disappeared for a while, which was unusual for her. I wondered what she was up to until I went out later and realised she had taken all the clothes off and hung them up again her special way. I don't know about you, people, but the clothes always dried when I hung the tops by the bottom and the bottoms by the top. Erin also refolded a basket full of clothes one day, as I had done that wrong too (or should I say, not her way). Stuff like that never bothered me; it was only the personal abuse that wore me down, and I felt I deserved better.

Nevertheless, the relationship continued, and we spent some wonderful quality time together, which allowed us both to understand each other better. There were times when I offered to help with her obvious issues, but she was always in denial, so I had to tread lightly.

I must have ended the relationship about a dozen times, but I kept going back for more. I knew in my heart that this wasn't going to be a lifelong partnership or that it might not even last out the year, but something or someone kept telling me that the lesson hadn't been learnt yet.

I had an unshakable faith in what was happening. It would have been easy for me to move away, change my phone number, and never see her again. I didn't want any easy way. For me to grow as a person, I wanted to endure the bad and the ugly as well as the good. I wanted to see the bad and the ugly as good. I didn't want to judge this person or the situation, only to experience it. After all, she was only reflecting back to me a part of myself that I couldn't yet see. It had to be something other than a mental illness, because I knew that I was travelling okay.

I read an article on mental illness and borderline personality disorder; I discovered that the description was that of Erin's behaviour. Halfway through the article, there was a line written in much larger font which read "You are not the crazy one." It was a trait of a person with this illness to always blame the other person and to convince them that they were the crazy one. I got such a relief upon reading that line. It changed everything for me. Knowing now that I was not the crazy one,

I could stand even more resolute in who I was, without feeling intimidated or belittled.

I decided to discuss with Erin the idea of moving in with her again and giving it a good go. It was a half-hearted attempt last time, as I'd only moved in a small amount of my stuff. I went all the way this time. I said to Evie on my way out that I was off to learn mastery.

The first three weeks were bliss, and I thought we'd turned the corner in our relationship. For some reason, Erin struggled to control her extreme personalities. I wanted to believe that I had done or said something to cause her rants, raves, and rages, but I monitored my behaviour very closely, and it just seemed that something would snap inside her head, and she would lose control. I couldn't understand, though, how Erin could put it all on to someone else. It was as though her subconscious was telling her that she was not worthy of this relationship, so she had to sabotage it, and to save face, it was not going to be her fault. There must have been an horrific programme running in her subconscious mind, and I was keen to find out a little more. I felt that her abandonment issues ran deep, and when the opportunity arose, I decided to ask her mother about Erin's childhood.

I humoured Erin for as long as possible when she took it upon herself to take me to six different people for therapy. I dared not refuse her offer but explained to most of the people what I was up against. I went to a priest who was a friend of hers and came to the conclusion that he needed more help than me. I went along to what would be my final meeting, but he never showed up. He did ring a few days later to apologise.

I also went to see a close lady friend of Erin's and told her of my MM and the issues I was having with Erin, explaining that I was trying to help her. I could tell that I blew this woman away with my stories. There was a male friend and another woman who were doing some spiritual work on me. This gave me an insight into the type of work spiritual people do. I went to see a reiki master, which I found absolutely amazing. I told Erin afterwards that if I ever did any spiritual healing work, it would be through this modality. Finally, I spoke to another of her friends, named Ben. I did tell you that she was in the know. I talked to Ben about our relationship and said I felt I was wasting his time. He was a very pleasant young fellow and was going through some relationship issues himself. I opened up about my MM and explained how it changed my whole way of thinking and living.

He calmly said, "Oh, wow, you've experienced a samadhi. That's a rare phenomenon."

"Is that what it was?" I asked.

"It sounds like it to me," he replied.

I had no idea what a samadhi was and wondered why nobody else picked up on it. I suppose I hadn't mentioned it to the right person before.

I want to finish my story on my relationship with Erin before I go into the details of a samadhi. I did have a bit of a chat to Erin's mum and found out enough to indicate why her blueprint was fear based. Erin's mum informed me that she had attempted to take Erin to seek help on several occasions over the years, but she always refused to go.

I decided for the sake of the relationship that I would force her into a corner, literally. I got her to sit in a chair in the corner of the bedroom and asked why she would not see someone about her condition. You can imagine her response, but I could see that she was just a frightened little girl. Erin could tell that I was not going to let up until we had sorted things out. I was aware at all times of her responses and had to give and take as we crawled towards a solution.

She eventually surrendered and started to talk about her illness and said that she was dealing with it her way. I wasn't sure if I was caught up in the middle of a sophisticated mind game or a genuine attempt to seek help. I offered to help as much as I could and suggested that we seek a professional for advice, which she agreed to.

The following day was a different matter, as she denied that she admitted to having a problem. She began to get even more nasty and resentful. I was okay with that, as I knew I had given it my best shot.

During our final week, my only words would be yes or no, depending on the question. I didn't want to elaborate on anything, as it would have been fodder for her abuse. I only had to stand in her presence for the relentless innuendo and criticism to come pouring from her mouth. I knew that she couldn't help it and understood that this was her way of protecting herself. I waited and waited, day by day, for seven days straight. I was emotionally drained and completely shattered.

On the Saturday, I decided I would give it till Sunday night, and if Erin was still in a dark place, I would have to move out on the Monday, without her knowing. I would not have been able to do it any other way.

I moved in with some mates, Jonathan and Dave, who just happened to have a spare bedroom at their place that suited me perfectly. I got a text from Erin late Monday afternoon, asking what time I would be home, as she had misplaced her front door key. I texted back to say that my key was on her pillow with a note and that I didn't live there anymore. I then turned my phone off.

Chapter 29

It wasn't until recently that I learned what the definition of a samadhi was. It'd been four and a half years since I had that conversation with Ben, but for some reason, I didn't think it necessary to do any research. It wasn't going to change what happened to me, and I was relieved that it had a name, and that I wasn't a freak. However, on doing the research, I wished I had done it ten years ago (having said that, though, I would not have been ready ten years ago). Something seemed to have been stopping me from delving into it too deeply. I think I was afraid of being led into some crazy religious sect or leaving my family and friends to live as a Buddhist monk in India or the Himalayas. As it turned out, religion never became an issue, and the many books I read on spirituality seemed to explain why. But, then, none mentioned samadhi, either.

I remember Erin dragging me to the library one day. She walked me down a particular aisle, randomly pulled out two books, and handed them to me. That evening, I read the first few pages from one of the books and was very interested in its information on spiritual experiences. I was particularly interested in the words that had been written in bold font throughout the pages. One word that caught my eye was *transient*. I put the book down so as only to prolong gratification. I wanted to savour it, so I decided to read the other book first.

This other book was called *Life and Teaching of the Masters of the Far East.*

One evening, I asked Erin, "What was it that made you grab these two books? You didn't even look at them."

Erin looked at me with a ridiculous smirk on her face and didn't say a word, which reminded me of Kat when I would ask seemingly simple questions. I let it go and kept reading.

By the time I finished reading *Life and Teaching of the Masters of the Far East*, both books were due back at the library, so I missed out on reading the first one. I thought that I would get it out another day, but when I went back, I couldn't find it (it didn't help that I'd forgotten the name of the book).

If I told you that throughout history, people had walked on water, time travelled, walked through solid walls, and lived to three hundred years old and beyond, would you believe me? It probably doesn't matter whether you believe it or not, but if you would like to, then I suggest you read *Life and Teaching of the Masters of the Far East.* Bloody bugger; I wish I could remember the name of that other book.

The many books I'd read and the different spiritual people I'd met were all confirmation that my MM was the real deal; as phenomenal as it was, I still struggled to comprehend the enormity of it. The fact that there was nobody there to take me by the hand and guide me through the aftermath was a let-down. That little boy in me was feeling insecure and frightened, thinking that everyone knew I was silly and were criticising me behind my back. At the same time, there was a driving force so powerful that I struggled to keep my feet on the ground. In fact, trying to stay a part of this so-called real world was very difficult. Knowing the truth and discovering the illusion meant that I was trying to survive in two very different worlds.

I believe I experienced a level of Savikalpa samadhi, which is a rare state of consciousness. I discovered that there were various kinds of samadhi. Among the minor samadhis, Savikalpa samadhi happens to be the highest. Beyond Savikalpa comes Nirvikalpa samadhi, but there is a great gulf between these two. There is something even beyond Nirvikalpa samadhi called Sahaja samadhi, but to save any confusion, I'll stay with the one I believe I experienced. Some say that it takes a lot of spiritual practise with deep meditation and years of yoga practise to achieve this state, and others say it can happen to anyone at any time. It is my view that it can happen to all of us, but the trigger for the event is unknown to me at this stage. The following is an excerpt from one of many websites that explain the samadhi experience.

In Savikalpa samadhi, there is both the bliss and the consciousness. One is fully engaged in samadhi; there is no awareness of outside surroundings. However, one remains aware that there is someone having an experience. The sense of personal identity still remains, albeit in a highly tenuous fashion.

When samadhi first occurs, there is a beginning of enlightenment. It takes a while for the impact of this samadhi to permeate your life, although the change is immediate and unmistakable. Over the ensuing months or years, this influence transforms all your life, every facet of who you are.

In Savikalpa samadhi, for a short period of time, you lose all human consciousness. In this state, the conception of time and space is altogether different. For an hour or two, you are completely in another world. You see there that almost everything is done. Here in this world, there are many desires still unfulfilled in oneself and in others. Millions of desires are not fulfilled, and millions of things remain to be done. But when you are in Savikalpa samadhi, you see that practically everything is done; you have nothing to do. You are only an instrument. If you are used, well and good; otherwise, things are all done. But from Savikalpa samadhi, everybody has to return to ordinary consciousness.

In Savikalpa samadhi, there are thoughts and ideas coming from various places, but they do not affect you. While you are meditating, you remain undisturbed, and your inner being functions in a dynamic and confident manner. You do the usual things that an ordinary human being does, but in the inmost recesses of your heart, you are charged with divine illumination.

I believe the first experience I had on the Sunday morning when Kat was with me was a Savikalpa samadhi, and I still can't explain the experience of the Holy Spirit the following evening. I don't believe I would have had the MM without having the cosmic travel experience on the Sunday.

Chapter 30

My stay at Jon and Dave's could only be described as a hibernation period, a time to reflect and to heal. I didn't go out socialising very often, and I always enjoyed my periods of celibacy and solitude. I was there about three months with no interest in making contact with Evie or Kelly; I guess as far as they knew, I was still living with Erin. I would spend most of my time in my downstairs bedroom, which had a bathroom and toilet, and the laundry was just down the hall. I would only go upstairs to either cook dinner or eat what someone else had cooked.

The other times, I would light up a candle, burn some incense, put on my meditation music, and lay on my bed. I was getting text messages all the time from Erin, but I ignored them. I was emotionally drained and decided to take all the time I needed to feel better again. These obvious periods of necessary pain never interfered with my work commitments or my physical and mental responsibilities. It's difficult to explain and hard to understand, but I felt these self-inflicted growing pains were necessary for me to gain a better understanding of who I was and what I was meant to be doing with him. I thought I'd self-realised many years ago, but as it has turned out, that was just a realisation of who I was not.

I finally made contact with Evie, and she allowed me to move back in with her. Being a transient person, it was always easy for me to move home at the drop of a hat. I only had the essentials, as all my furniture was put into storage when I moved from the rented house about eighteen months earlier. There was nothing more to gain staying at Jon and Dave's, and I needed a like-minded person to talk to. Evie also liked company and someone to talk to, and I was a good listener.

I had only been at Evie's a couple of weeks when one evening, as we were finishing dinner, I received a text from Liz, asking if I'd like to have dinner with her. Liz was the daughter of Bob, an old friend of mine; at the time, I'd known them for almost thirty years. A week earlier, I had been over to Bob's place for dinner, and Liz happened to be there. She had asked me if I was in a relationship, and I told her I was not. She was twelve years my junior, and therefore, it never occurred to me that she was interested in going out.

Dating was the last thing on my mind, so when I read the text, I started shaking my head, thinking, *Here we go again.*

I showed Evie the text and asked, "What should I do?"

"That's your decision, my friend, not mine," she replied.

I decided that it was all beyond my control and arranged to meet her.

I started to ponder the seven matchsticks that I had left over from the poker game as a teenager. Maybe I miscounted, or maybe a brother nicked a couple, or some fell on the floor. Either way, I ended up with more girlfriends than I ever imagined or anticipated. I thought I was dealing with the situation quite well, contrary to what my mother believed.

Mum passed away during my relationship with Erin, and it was a very emotional time, especially since my father was in a secure dementia ward at an aged care facility. There was also an issue with Sarah; my sister seemed to be going a little crazy with a delusional disorder. They all ended up in the same hospital at the same time, which was the result of a visit to their home one afternoon. Mum was lying on her bed, looking very ill, while Sarah was floating around somewhere. Dad, in his state of dementia, came in and lay on the bed beside Mum. He started to complain about a problem down there, pointing to his groin area. He had suffered a stroke many years prior, and I was beginning to think that he may be having another. I started to prod his stomach area and his hips and thighs, but I could see he was getting exasperated. He suddenly pulled his shorts down and exposed himself, saying, "There, there."

I started prodding the area while asking, "Is it here or there? What do you feel?"

He got even more exasperated and pulled his shorts back up. I looked at my mother, but she just shrugged her shoulders, as if she didn't give a damn. I was thinking that this was ridiculous and something needed to be done.

As it turned out, Dad was taken to hospital during the following week, and when I visited Mum afterwards, I knew it was time for her as well. I rang my eldest brother Richard, and told him that I was ringing an ambulance for our mother, and I didn't think she'd be coming back home.

It wasn't long before Sarah's delusional disorder got the better of her, which also disturbed my brother Phil, who lived in the granny flat out the back. Sarah would ring triple zero at midnight because she thought she could hear blood-curdling screams next door. The only option available was for Sarah to stay in hospital until an appropriate place was found for her. She spent six months in the children's ward of this hospital. During this time, I found out how vital social workers are within the system.

The episode with Dad on the bed was still haunting me when I suddenly remembered Richard telling me one day that Mum had said that Dad had been impotent since retirement twenty years earlier. My father, in his state of dementia, was trying to tell me of his dilemma, which had obviously been a great source of frustration for him over many years. I felt a deep sadness come over me but then let it go.

I don't know what you're thinking at this stage, people, but you are probably wondering why a relationship with another woman would have anything to do with saving the world. I didn't know, either, but what I did know was that intimate relationships were good for my personal development and growth. I was able to enter a zone of awareness that would allow me to be as close as possible to the truth of who I was. My vulnerable side would be exposed, as well as the love that I was willing to show and share. This would allow the relationship to blossom very quickly, and we would be taken into a world beyond the mundane.

The fact that this lady was similar to but not the same as Erin and Faye led me to believe that there was definitely something that I was not seeing in myself. Should I tell you that there was something different about this woman that I just couldn't put my finger on? There were signs of obsessive, possessive, and compulsive behaviour that I'd become accustomed to, but the cunning manipulation was something that I had risen above.

As we got deeper into a loving relationship, I soon realised that I was not the man for Liz, so I explained to her that the relationship had to end, and that I wanted to be on my own. I was ready to embark on a long period of celibacy. As upset as Liz was, we would remain friends, as we'd always been.

It wasn't long before I eventually gave into Erin's requests to meet and talk. Erin never gave up, and I met with her a few times, if only to confirm that we were done and that we would just be friends. At what I thought would be our last meeting, Erin asked if I would chaperone her to a dinner for her daughter's birthday party, but I was hesitant and said that I would let her know. The party was the same evening that Liz had invited me over, as she had some musician friends who were coming over to jam. I wasn't sure which to attend or if I should bother with either. I should have known that the decision was never mine to make.

Two nights before the events, I was discussing with Evie which way I should go. Just as we were talking about it, a text came through from Erin to say that the birthday dinner had been cancelled. Almost immediately, I got a revelation that I would meet my next lover at Liz's party. At the same time, I realised that I would have gone to the birthday dinner had it not been cancelled.

"She must be very special," I said to Evie. "There goes my celibacy."

I had no doubt that I would meet a woman on this evening and that she would be nothing like the triple treat I'd just endured: Faye, Erin, and Liz.

This was a perfect example of letting go and allowing the outside forces to guide me. It was much better and safer than trying to take control and use my so-called better judgement, which would come from a programmed mind that I was still trying to tame. As the description of a samadhi goes, you see that practically everything is done; you have nothing to do. You are only an instrument. If you are used, well and good; otherwise, things are all done.

Enough had happened in my life since I experienced the samadhi and MM to make me think that anything in this world was possible. There was an outside force, an energy source far beyond one's comprehension that seemed to be more in control than one imagined. I believed that I had tapped into this arena when I went cosmic flying that Sunday morning with Kat many years ago. It was as if I was in this world but not of this world; we are all in the same boat. I wanted to learn more, so I allowed myself to be driven by this unseen force, no matter where it took me. I had to believe that these extraordinary relationships were all part of a master plan that would soon be exposed. I was also hoping that the women were getting a lot out of the experience as well.

Speaking of that Sunday morning with the so-called Kundalini awakening that Kat mentioned, I did some research, and this is what I found: There is a pathway in the body, which is mainly connected to the spine and which is called Kunda. When the life force flows through, it is named Kundalini. This precious pathway unites us between earth and sky, matter and spirit, body and no-body. When the Kundalini stays at the level of the sexual organs and sexual activity, it carries a certain vibration. The more it is elevated in the Kunda channel, the more our inner vibration changes. The happy vibration of sex becomes a vibration of joy in the heart. Then sex feels like a divine experience. Sex and love are integrated in the same action.

This is a very powerful process that totally transforms our way of life. Once you taste the joy of love embracing the body, life takes a different direction. However, Kundalini flow does not only create new sexual experiences. It embraces much more than that. It activates our capacity for unity with everything in life. Kundalini supports us in being in this embrace all the time, not just during sexual intercourse. It shifts the experience of unity to everything around: the trees, the flowers, the moon, the sky full of stars.

At the same time, it creates a lot of changes on the bodily level. The vibration of our cells, brain, organs, and blood flow is activated to a new level of light. It nourishes and rejuvenates our entire organism and awakens the capacity of our body to live life fully.

Kundalini carries the quality of unity. In expression, it can be silent, motionless, and yet expressive. It all depends on what the Kundalini encounters on its way through you. If there is fear, you can be sure that fear will be actively expressed. If there is happiness, it will come shining through equally. It is important to understand that Kundalini is exposing everything hidden inside us, fear as much as joy. Kundalini is a non-dual energy that always looks for union. If there is something in the way of unity, it will be exposed so that it can be dropped or transformed. This is the powerful beauty of Kundalini: It is a healing, transformative force which awakens us to unity. It calls us back to our state of oneness.

Further to this, I can only surmise that the joy and bliss that I was feeling at the time of my awakening was a factor in the Kundalini energy or life force being released through the pathway in my body.

Here is more on the subject: Kundalini is dormant within most people. In Hindu mythology, Kundalini is a serpent goddess who lies asleep at the base of the spine, coiled three and a half times around the first chakra. Her name is Kundalini Shakti, and she represents the unfolding of the divine Shakti energy, the energizing potential of life itself, a living goddess who enlivens all things.

Under certain circumstances, the Kundalini energy awakens and begins to rise through the body, piercing and opening the chakras as she moves in her undulating, snake-like fashion. As Kundalini releases stored and blocked energies, her movement can be quite intense, sometimes painful, and often leads to mental states that seem out of this world.

Circumstances that stimulate Kundalini awakening are many and varied; they are usually triggered by such things as extended periods of meditation, yoga, fasting, stress, trauma, psychedelic drugs, or near-death experiences.

Kundalini is a condensed, primal force, similar to the potential energy found in water. When released, it creates a vertical connection between the chakras by opening the subtle channels known as *nadi*, most specifically, the central channel that moves up the spine called *sushumna*. If we put water through a small hose at very high pressure, the end of the hose will undulate like a snake. Similarly, the intense energy of Kundalini undulates in the body as it rises through the chakras.

Kundalini can also be seen as a result of the chakras connecting to each other. Theoretically, as the chakras enlarge, the spinning of one can enhance the spinning of the one above or below it. Kundalini is basically a healing force.

With the experience of the Kundalini awakening followed by the Samadhi, no wonder it felt like I was out of this world. I still feel cosmic in nature and one with all things, including God. Now that's another story. Oh, why not? Not long after my samadhi and MM, I had another short but extraordinary experience. It was instantly revealed to me as a God realisation. This is a very difficult thing to describe, so I hope you bear with me.

I felt a flow of energy enter through the top of my head. It was a mass of a divine nature that left no doubt that God was real, present, and within me and about me. It was like God saying, "Hello, you are a part of me, and I am a part of you. We are one, and we are one with all things." If I had any doubt before, I now knew what oneness meant.

Now come on, people, if I'd told you this at the beginning of the book, you would've given up on me and missed out on all that fabulous reading. Besides, this is not about God; this is about our minds and the energy force that our minds have control over (or is that the other way around?). Do you want to know how we are to save the world or not? You're probably more interested in the Friday-night jam session I'm about to attend and the new lover I'm about to meet. Don't be so shallow, people.

Chapter 31

I arrived early, as did a girlfriend of Liz's. She was very attractive, and as I listened to the two women converse, I soon became aware that she was not for me. Am I teasing you, or was the universe teasing me? I let it go and decided that this was ridiculous, so I looked up at the universe and said, "You are not connecting me with a woman tonight, and I'll be leaving without meeting anyone." I wanted to test the power of the force.

As I met and mingled with people, nibbling the food and topping up my drink, I drifted off into thought. I wondered how I got into this situation and where it was all leading me to. How could I get off this roller-coaster ride and find some normality in my life? I'd just broken up with Liz, and here I was at her place, waiting to meet my next adventure. Not only that; I'd told Liz that I wanted to be on my own for a while and not be in a relationship. How was the universe going to pull this one off?

I have always enjoyed live music, not just because of the music itself, but because of the skills shown by the people playing the instruments. It was definitely something I would have liked in my repertoire. Okay, so I fantasised about being a rock star.

It was getting late in the evening when a few more guests arrived. A couple who seemed to know everybody walked in, and behind them in the darkness was another couple. When the dust settled and the fog cleared, a lone woman was revealed. As soon as I saw her, I knew she was the one but was determined not to get involved.

Liz then called me over to meet her friends: "James, I want you to meet Don and Sal."

We shook hands, and then they in turn introduced me to the lady who appeared from the darkness behind them: "This is our friend Cheryl."

I shared pleasantries and other small talk, and then went back to the party to mingle.

Suddenly, everyone sat quietly to listen to a couple play and sing. I took the opportunity to go inside for a drink; when I returned, Liz was in the seat I'd vacated. I looked around for another, and the only one available was next to Cheryl. As I paused for a moment to think about the irony of that, I decided that I had no choice but to sit by her.

Should I tell you now that there was something different about this woman that I just couldn't put my finger on? Should I tell you that there was so much energy between us that I could feel sparks fly? I had tried to avoid her from the moment she walked in. Even whilst sitting together, we hardly spoke, but it didn't matter; I knew where we were going. As she was leaving, her friend Sal insisted we exchange phone numbers. Should I tell you that on their departure, I gave Cheryl a warm hug and a kiss on the lips? Here I go again.

As I sit here and write this book nearly four and a half years after that evening, I can say that I am still with this extraordinary woman. I hear you cheer, and I thank you. You have to trust in the universe (or you can say God, if you want to). You are probably thinking why I should continue writing if I don't have any more women to write about. You're being shallow again. You and I still have work to do, people, so don't fall asleep on me.

The roller coaster slowed to a crawl, and life became more normal (well, as normal as it can be for someone like me). My family and friends were impressed with my new-found stability. I wasn't fooled, though, and knew there was more than meets the eye, wink wink. My relationship with several was over, but my relationship with myself had only just begun.

I lived with the knowing that everything changes and nothing stays the same; having to hold on to something like this has been a challenge, particularly when I was so used to letting go so often. Knowing the unique and perfect serendipity that the universe orchestrated to form this relationship, it was clear to me that I was not going anywhere, and whatever the reason for me being here would be revealed soon enough.

It wasn't long before I started to feel vulnerable, frightened, and insecure. I felt myself changing while everything else was staying the same. I was feeling emotions that I hadn't experienced for such a long time, even from childhood. There was jealousy, longing, abandonment, and resentment: all silly things that I was struggling to control. I didn't understand why because these things had never been an issue in the past, or if they were, it never affected me this way.

One day, about eighteen months into the relationship, while relaxing on the lounge chair, I received an amazing and enlightening revelation (this was the same lounge chair I was sitting on when I realised my greatness and my genius). This profound new revelation was both liberating and a horrible realisation that shocked me to the core. In a matter of seconds, a movie of my life played out. I watched my behaviour, my moods, my outbursts, my manipulation, my fear, and all the ramifications of trying to be in control. I realised that all my life, I had been battling mental illness.

In that instant, I realised that depression was in fact a mental illness, something you could not have convinced me of before then. I realised I had been in denial all my life, and suddenly, everything made sense. The way I treated people, the way I spoke to them, the resentment, anger, bitterness, criticism, judgement, and deception all played out, seemingly right in front of my eyes. I thought immediately that I wanted to go back and make up for the wrongs, but I knew it was too late. I felt shame and regret; I wanted to apologise for everything and wanted to take it all back, if given a chance. On the other side of the scale, I had to be thankful for the realisation and grateful that I'd learnt the truth.

I had to reassess where I was at. Who was I now? Am I still that narcissistic, sarcastic, arrogant man? Actually, I wasn't that bad; it was only on occasions when my buttons were pushed or the stress and anxiety took over.

I had changed so much since my samadhi; I didn't think I was still operating from that blueprint. I thought of my relationships with Fay, Erin, and Liz and saw them as being a mirror of myself. There was no way anyone could have convinced me of that prior to this revelation. I now know why these relationships had to happen; they led me to this awakening. I now understand how I attracted them into my life. However, I don't believe I've had an issue since my samadhi, as I had become very conscious of my thoughts, words, and actions from that moment. Still, I wasn't sure anymore. Did this mean I had to become even more aware? Was I to delve even deeper into my subconscious to expose more hidden surprises?

I remember zooming in on that little boy full of fear and anxiety, troubled and confused, shy and self-conscious, angry, disillusioned, and frustrated, the black sheep of the family. What happened to me? Why was I like this? Why was it necessary to prove myself all the time, protect myself?

I was the perfect fear being, with the negative blueprint attached to my subconscious. I will never know what happened to me to create such a fearful existence, but it doesn't matter anymore. All I know is that it can be remedied if the right tools are implemented. I have been able to overcome the anger and resentment I've carried since childhood and replaced it with love and forgiveness, which I might add is the key to liberation. Forgiveness is the scent of the violet upon the heel that has crushed it.

It's been three years since that frightening revelation, and I'm still coming to terms with it all. And yes, I'm still in a loving relationship with Cheryl. The experience of the samadhi and the awareness of a mental illness have both enlightened my world during that time. The combination has given me amazing insights, though, into human behaviour and the human psyche and a wonderful understanding of all types of relationships. At any given time, I can pause to assess where I am at psychologically. Am I anxious, am I depressed, am I a love being or in a state of fear? Which programme is running through my mind at the moment? I am no longer in denial and well aware of my limitations and, of course, my limitlessness. I have become an observer and the master of my own mind.

My purpose now is to inform, educate, inspire, and save the world. It sounds a bit crazy to me. What do you think?

Chapter 32

It's obvious that I discovered my spiritual nature all those years ago. I could have said that I am a spiritual person, but as I mentioned before, we are all spiritual. We have been programmed to focus on the physical and mental attributes of our being and have let go of the very essence of who we are. If the truth be known, we are spiritual beings having a human experience.

I've spent most of my life, as many others have, wondering what it was that was missing. There must be more to it than this, I would think. Having a wife and a family and all the material wealth, good friends, great job was all wonderful, but the search was still going on. I now know exactly what it was and feel blessed to have discovered that part of me that was missing for so long. I tell you this: if you haven't discovered your spiritual essence, and you are telling yourself that you feel complete, then you are in denial.

The irony is that the essence of who you are is all you need to know. Everything else is taken care of: one's health, both physical and mental, one's lifestyle, relationships, finances, and education. It's all about perceptions and acceptance. Remember, practically everything is done; you have nothing to do. You are only an instrument. If you are used, then well and good; otherwise, things are all done. This is not something that everyone will understand, but I have written it for those who want to learn more about their true essence.

Our true essence is love; we are love. I know this. I feel this. Love is all we are, for only love is real. All else are illusions. There's a Sanskrit saying that goes "Everything that is, isn't, and everything that isn't, is."

These simple truths are buried inside us all. People go out into the world searching, but all that needs doing is to lift the veil of deception by going inward. Rumi said, "There is a voice that doesn't use words. Listen."

Not long after I experienced my MM, I felt the need to sit in silence, to be on my own in my sanctuary of love and just listen. There is another dimension that talks to us when we are in silence. This was, of course, meditation, and I found myself doing a lot of it. I was fortunate that my mind was calm. I had nothing to concern myself with.

Take the first step, people. Come with me on this sometimes-arduous journey, this extraordinary trek into the truth. You will not be disappointed. There is no place on earth that comes close to the panorama you'll find within. Take up your vantage point and make it your advantage point.

The best and probably only way to listen to that wordless voice is through meditation, and it is highly recommended by Jimmy Digne. It's like listening to a reverent whisper, the voice of your soul.

There are many people on their spiritual path, searching for the truth, and there are many levels of awareness or consciousness.

I have realised the truth; the search is over for me, but the learning still goes on. I am learning things I already knew but had forgotten. In fact, we are on this earth to remember all that is already known to us but have forgotten. We are born with the truth, but unfortunately, too many of us die with the lies.

Most of the world is non compos mentis or in a slumber, that is, unaware of their true self, their spiritual essence, their greatness, their genius; they will struggle to assist us in saving the world. If you know someone like that, please give them this book to read (or you may have to read it to them). They need to know that we cannot save the world with a gun or a crucifix. It cannot be saved with money, politics, or war. We cannot make laws, set rules and regulations, or charge fees, fines, rates, or tolls just to make this a better or safer world. If anything, these things exacerbate the problems of the world.

It's all about individuals taking responsibility for everything that happens in the world, not just in their lives. That doesn't mean we all have to travel the world, sorting out other people's issues. Realising the truth of who we are will allow us to see the world as it really is, which in turn will allow us to create a better world. It is impossible for us to be everywhere in the world at once, but if we see ourselves as the world, and if we are the change that we want to see, then we have a better chance of making this a better world. I am the world. You are the world. We are the world.

Chapter 33

I think that last chapter was a summary of how it is possible to save the world. If I can be more specific in this chapter, then we may all get a better understanding of what we need to do, including myself.

There is no doubt that knowledge of self is a vital piece of the puzzle, as knowing that our external world is a reflection of our internal world can be very powerful. Self-knowledge allows us to see the illusion that our mind has created through being conditioned all our lives. If we reprogramme our mind with positive and loving thoughts, then we will see the world in a different light. If we want the world to be a beautiful place, then we have to see ourselves as beautiful. We all need to change our view of ourselves on a deeper level. We need to love ourselves right to the core and then project this core essence outwards; no words, no thoughts, no deeds, just feel love and be love.

If we all suddenly woke up to ourselves and realised the truth of who we are, then something as simple as mass consciousness would change the world in an instant. Leo Tolstoy said, "Everyone thinks of changing the world but no one thinks of changing himself." Another quote from Rumi: "Yesterday I was clever, so I wanted to change the world; today I am wise, so I am changing myself."

Our culture needs a shakeup, and this can only happen through the nurturing of our children in ways that are conducive to their identity of self. I deliberately used nurturing, as programming, conditioning, or even our archaic system of educating will not create a whole person. A whole person is spiritually aware, aware of self. That's it. Everything else falls into place.

I am okay in my world; it is your world that worries me. What you put out, you get back. If you are not happy and always complaining about the world and its people, then guess what? That is your world, and you are responsible for what you have created. If you influence enough people, then they will do the same. If you influence children, then the wheel just keeps turning. It's time to get off the merry-go-round and fly like a bird.

Another quote from Rumi: "You were born with wings; why prefer to crawl through life?" There are no excuses. Intention is a powerful thing, and the art of manifestation is at your fingertips (or in the palm of your hand).

We are very powerful entities with enormous depth. If the law of attraction is used in a positive way, then all things can be achieved. We are as deep as the universe is vast, and there is a frontier out there, in here, that is beyond comprehension. I know. I've experienced it.

You can call me a dreamer, a light worker, a mystic, even an indigo child. Label me anything you want, but to all you realists out there, we have to start somewhere and start very soon. The universe is in a hurry, remember.

Chapter 34

It's time now for James Semper Digne to sign off; I may never come back to this reality. Hopefully, you will all start to do the work, which I might add is probably much easier than the work you are doing now. Everything changes, nothing stays the same, so let go, and don't hold onto to all those outdated and unnecessary false beliefs you have around who you are. You are love, and you are powerful and worthy of all that this magical world has to offer.

There is nothing outside yourself that can satisfy you as much as what is inside you. There is no need to change your job, unless you wish; there is no need to change where you live, unless you wish; there is no need to change your partner, unless you wish. Keep your car, your house, your boat, and all your material possessions and obsessions. When you delve deep within yourself and find the magic that resides, your materialistic world will pale into insignificance. Just sit back, relax, and watch the mystery, magic, and miracles unfold before your very eyes. This is the advantage point that you have been looking for all your life, and the world will be a better place for it.

With a smile on my face and water welling in my eyes, I say goodbye and wish you all the best. I love you. I have to. I am love.

James Semper Digne

(*Semper Digne*: Latin for "Always Worthy")

Printed in the United States
By Bookmasters